About Reading Connection:

Welcome to RBP Books' Connection series. Reading Connection provides students with focused practice to help reinforce and develop reading skills in areas appropriate for second-grade students. Reading Connection uses a variety of writing types and exercises to help build comprehension, thinking, phonics, vocabulary, language, reasoning, and other skills important to both reading and critical thinking. In accordance with NCTE (National Council of Teachers of English) standards, reading material and exercises are grade-level appropriate, and clear examples and instructions guide the lesson. Activities help students develop reading skills and give special attention to vocabulary development.

D1360791

Dear Parents and Educators,

Thank you for choosing this Rainbow Bridge Publishing educational product to help teach your children and students. We take great pride and pleasure in becoming involved with your educational experience. Some people say that math will always be math and reading will always be reading, but we do not share that opinion. Reading, math, spelling, writing, geography, science, history, and all other subjects will always be some of life's most fulfilling adventures and should be taught with passion both at home and in the classroom. Because of this, we at Rainbow Bridge Publishing associate the greatness of learning with every product we create.

It is our mission to provide materials that not only explain, but also amaze; not only review, but also encourage; not only guide, but also lead. Every product contains clear, concise instructions, appropriate sample work, and engaging, grade-appropriate content created by classroom teachers and writers that is based on national standards to support your best educational efforts. We hope you enjoy our company's products as you embark on your adventure. Thank you for bringing us along.

Sincerely,

George Starks
Associate Publisher
Rainbow Bridge Publishing

Reading Connection™ • Grade 2
Written by Nancy Bosse

Publisher
Scott G. Van Leeuwen

Associate Publisher
George Starks

Series Creator
Michele Van Leeuwen

Illustrations
Amanda Sorensen

Visual Design and Layout
Andy Carlson, Robyn Funk, Zachary Johnson,
Dante J. Orazzi

Editorial Director
Paul Rawlins

Copy Editors and Proofreaders
Kim Carlson, Lori Davis, Suzie Ellison, Melody Feist, Linda Swain

Please visit our website at
www.summerbridgeactivities.com
for supplements, additions, and corrections to this book.

Second Edition 2004

For orders call 1-800-598-1441
Discounts available for quantity orders

ISBN: 1-887923-81-0

PRINTED IN THE UNITED STATES OF AMERICA
10 9 8 7 6 5 4 3 2

Table of Contents

Sounds and Letters Chart

r(a)t   j(ar)   (b)ear   (c)at   (d)eer

(e)lephant   s(ea)l   f(er)n   (f)ish   (g)orilla

(h)orse   (i)nchworm   crocod(ile)   b(ir)d   (j)aguar

(k)angaroo   (kn)ot   (l)ion   (m)ouse   (n)ewt

go(ng)   (O)ctopus   g(oo)se   cl(ou)d   (p)ig

qu(a)il   (r)abbit   (s)un   (sh)ark   (t)urtle

(th)in   d(u)ck   vult(ur)e   (v)ase   (w)olf

(wh)ale   fo(x)   (y)ak   pon(y)   (z)ebra

2nd Grade Reading List

Adler, David
Cam Jansen and the Mystery of the
Dinosaur Bones

Allard, Harry
Miss Nelson books

Andersen, Hans Christian
The Emperor's New Clothes

Barracca, Debra
The Adventures of Taxi Dog

Berenstain, Stan & Jan
The Berenstain Bears books

Bond, Michael
Paddington Bear Series

Byars, Betsy Cromer
Hooray for the Golly Sisters!
The Golly Sisters Go West
The chapter books

Caudill, Rebecca
A Pocketful of Cricket

Coerr, Eleanor
Chang's Paper Pony

Cole, Joanna
Big Goof and Little Goof

Cushman, Doug
Aunt Eater's Mystery Vacation

Delton, Judy
Pee Wee Scout books

Flack, Marjorie
The Story about Ping

Funny Side Up books
Dinosaur Jokes
Knock, Knock Jokes
School Jokes
Space Jokes
Sports Jokes

Gackenbach, Dick
Mag the Magnificent

Griffith, Helen V.
Alex and the Cat

Hoban, Lillian
Arthur books

Hoff, Syd
The Horse in Harry's Room

Holabird, Katharine
Angelina Ballerina

Honeycutt, Natalie
The All New Jonah Twist

Hutchins, Pat
Don't Forget the Bacon

Jonas, Ann
Aardvarks, Disembark!

Keats, Ezra Jack
John Henry: An American Legend
Maggie and the Pirate

Kessler, Leonard P.
Here Comes the Strikeout

Kimmel, Eric A.
The Chanukkah Guest

2nd Grade Reading List

Komaiko, Leah
Annie Bananie

Kuskin, Karla
Soap Soup

Leaf, Munro
The Story of Ferdinand

Lexau, Joan M.
Striped Ice Cream

Lobel, Arnold
The Frog and Toad series

Mayer, Mercer
Just Me books

McCully, Emily Arnold
Zaza's Big Break

McDermott, Gerald
The Stonecutter

Miles, Miska
Annie and the Old One

Mozelle, Shirley
Zack's Alligator

O'Connor, Jane
Super Cluck
The Teeny Tiny Woman

Pickett, Anola
Old Enough for Magic

Platt, Kin
Big Max

Rey, H. A.
The Curious George series

Schwartz, Alvin
Busy Buzzing Bumblebees and
Other Tongue Twisters
There Is a Carrot in My Ear and
Other Noodle Tales
In a Dark, Dark Room and
Other Scary Stories
All of Our Noses are Here and
Other Noodle Stories
I Saw You in the Bathtub and
Other Folk Rhymes

Sharmat, Marjorie Weinman
A Big, Fat Enormous Lie

Sharmat, Mitchell
Gregory, the Terrible Eater

Small, David
Imogene's Antlers

Steig, William
The Zabajaba Jungle

Titus, Eve
Anatole books

Waber, Bernard
Bernard

Zion, Gene
Harry by the Sea

The Library

I am a library, and through my door
Are shelves of books and so much more.

Through my doors, adventures are free,
So please come in, but quietly.

My books can take you to outer space,
Deep into the ocean, or anyplace.

Read my books and you will see
What the world can really be.

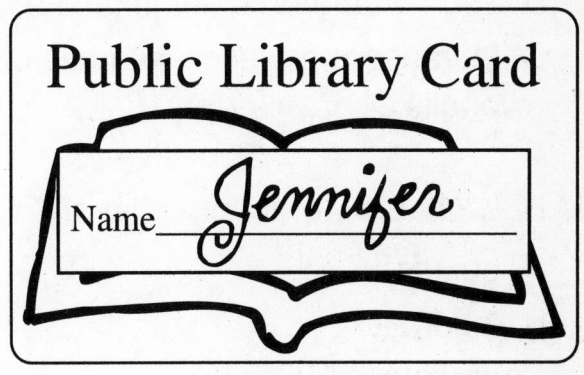

Public Library Card

Name____Jennifer

© RBP Books   www.summerbridgeactivities.com   Reading Connection—Grade 2—RBP3810

Reading Skills

1. What is the main idea of the poem?

    A. Reading takes a lot of practice.

    B. You have to be quiet in a library.

    C. Libraries are places with lots of books.

2. How should we go into a library?

    A. quietly

    B. loudly

    C. on tiptoes

3. According to the poem, where can books take you?

    A. to the library shelves

    B. through the library doors

    C. anyplace

Thinking Skills

1. The poem says, "...through my door, are shelves of books and so much more." Put a √ by the things you could find in a library.

    _____ computer

    _____ maps

    _____ basketball hoop

    _____ video tapes

    _____ encyclopedias

    _____ couch

Vocabulary Skills

Write a word from the poem that rhymes with each word below. Then think of a word of your own that rhymes.

1. door _____ _____

2. free _____ _____

3. space _____ _____

4. see _____ _____

Language Skills

Circle the correct **past tense** form.

1. I <u>read</u> lots of books. (present tense)

    I (read   readed) lots of books.
    (past tense)

2. I <u>see</u> the books on the shelf.
   (present tense)

    I (seed   saw) the books on the shelf.
    (past tense)

3. I <u>take</u> the books home.
   (present tense)

    I (took   taked) the books home.
    (past tense)

4. Please, <u>come</u> in. (present tense)

    I (comed   came) in.
    (past tense)

The Snowman

It was a snowy day. Braxton and Hayden decided to make a snowman. They bundled up and ran outside. First, they rolled a great big snowball for the body. Then they rolled a medium-sized snowball for the middle. Finally, they rolled a small snowball for the head. They stacked the three snowballs together. They found rocks for his eyes and mouth. They found a pinecone for his nose. They used sticks for his arms. They were proud of their snowman when they finished.

www.summerbridgeactivities.com Reading Connection—Grade 2—RBP3810

Reading Skills

1. What is the main idea?

A. making a snowman

B. playing in the snow

C. making a snow angel

2. Number the sentences in the order that they happen in the story.

_____ They rolled a medium-sized snowball.

_____ They found rocks for his eyes and mouth.

_____ They rolled a great big snowball.

_____ They rolled a small snowball for the head.

_____ They stacked the snowballs.

3. What season is it?

A. winter

B. spring

C. fall

Vocabulary Skills

Write the two words that make up each **compound word**.

1. snowman _____ _____

2. snowball _____ _____

3. pinecone _____ _____

4. outside _____ _____

Language Skills

Write the correct **plural** form for each noun.

1. day _____

2. snowman _____

3. stick _____

4. snowball _____

5. pinecone _____

Thinking Skills

1. What is your favorite season?

_____

Write three things you like to do during that season.

_____

_____

_____

Come to the Meadow

Come to the meadow where the primrose grows,
Daisies and cowslips lined up in rows.

Buttercups looking as yellow as gold,
Truly it is a sight to behold.

Busy bees humming about them are seen.
Grasshoppers chirp in the tall grasses so green.

Butterflies happily fluttering along,
The bluebirds are singing a lively new song.

So come to the meadow and there you'll see
Spring come alive for you and for me.

www.summerbridgeactivities.com   **Reading Connection—Grade 2—RBP3810**

Reading Skills

1. What is the main idea?

    A. The meadow is pretty in spring.

    B. Bees are busy insects.

    C. Bluebirds like to sing.

2. What sings a lively song?

    A. grasshoppers

    B. bees

    C. bluebirds

3. Which of these is not a flower?

    A. buttercup

    B. butterfly

    C. cowslip

Vocabulary Skills

1. Draw a line between the rhyming words.

grows	green
gold	rows
seen	me
along	behold
see	song

2. What does <u>behold</u> mean?

    A. to catch

    B. to draw

    C. to see

Language Skills

Write the **singular** form of the words below.

1. daisies _____

2. bees _____

3. butterflies _____

4. buttercups _____

5. grasses _____

Thinking Skills

Cross out the word that does not belong in each group.

1. primrose   daisy
    cowslip   oak tree

2. bee   grasses
    grasshopper   butterfly

3. humming   fluttering
    singing   meadow

Tulips

In my flower garden, tulips always grow,
Straight like toy soldiers all in a row.

With colors so bright, reds, oranges, yellows, too.
They are one of nature's special gifts just for you.

Their colorful petals shaped like a cup
Hold the little raindrops for birds to drink up.

Winds cause them to sway
Back and forth each day.

But still my tulips grow
Like toy soldiers in a row.

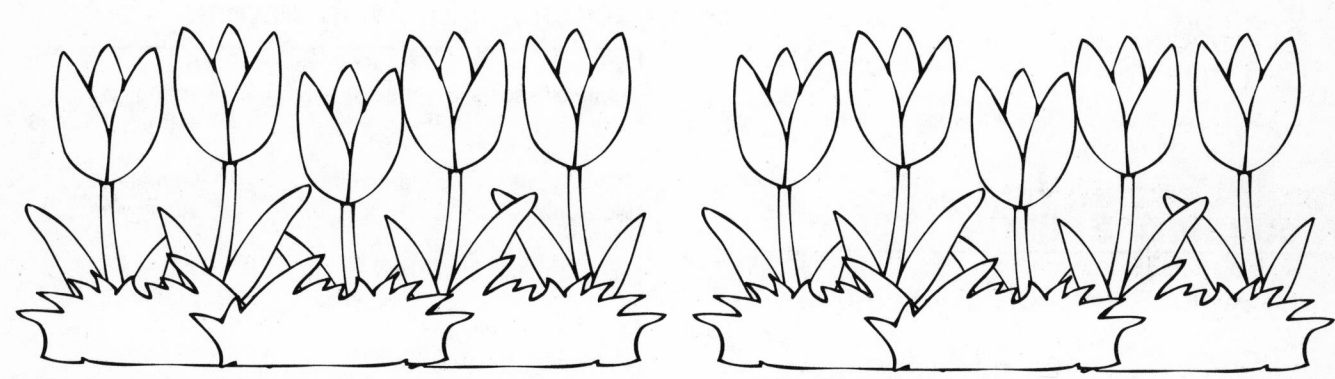

www.summerbridgeactivities.com   Reading Connection—Grade 2—RBP3810

Reading Skills

1. What is the poem about?

   A. flower gardens

   B. tulips

   C. toy soldiers

2. What are the tulips compared to?

   A. toy soldiers

   B. rainbow

   C. raindrops

3. What are the petals of the tulip shaped like?

   A. toy soldiers

   B. a cup

   C. a thimble

Vocabulary Skills

1. What does the word <u>sway</u> mean?

   A. grow

   B. move back and forth

   C. break

2. Find the *r-controlled* words in the poem. Place them in the correct group.

<u>or</u> words

_____

_____

_____

<u>ir</u> word

_____

<u>er</u> word

_____

<u>ar</u> words

_____

_____

Study Skills

Look at the index below from the back of a book about flowers. Write the page where you could find information on each of the following flowers.

A	H I J	S
apple blossoms 37	iris 8	spring 15
aster 62		stamen. 6, 7
	K L	stigma 6, 7
B	larkspur 47	summer 16
blossoms 13	lily 42	sunflowers 17
buttercups 65		
	M N	T U
C	marigolds. 29	thistle. 27
chrysanthemum 23		tulips 26
cowslips. 25	O P Q	
	pansies 31	V W
D E	petals. 6	violet 22
daffodil. 27	pistil. 6, 7	winter. 15
daisy 15		wisteria 20
	R	
F G	rose 19	X Y Z
fall 30		zinnia. 60
gardens 2		
gladiola 7		

1. tulips _____

2. pansies _____

3. daisies _____

4. roses _____

The Rain

Pitter patter, pitter pat…
How I love the rain!

Storm clouds moving in,
The rain is about to begin.
How I love to see the rain!

Tiny sprinkles on my face,
Little droplets playing chase.
How I love to feel the rain!

I open up my mouth so wide,
Letting little drops inside.
How I love to taste the rain!

Tapping on my window,
It's a rhythm that I know.
How I love to hear the rain!

Everything looks so green
And the fresh air smells so clean.
How I love to smell the rain!

Pitter patter, pitter pat…
How I love the rain!

Reading Skills

1. What is the main idea of the poem?
   A. reasons not to like rain
   B. reasons to like the rain
   C. why storms can be scary

2. Draw a line from the sense to what the writer of the poem loves about the rain.

   sight   tapping on the window

   touch   storm clouds moving in

   taste   little drops inside my mouth

   sound   tiny sprinkles on my face

   smell   fresh air

Vocabulary Skills

Find a word in the poem that rhymes with the word in the list. Write the word on the line.

1. begin _____

2. face _____

3. wide _____

4. window_____

5. green _____

Language Skills

Add the suffix **-ing** to each word.

1. move _____

2. play _____

3. let_____

4. tap _____

Thinking Skills

1. How does the writer of the poem feel about rain?

   _____

   _____

   _____

Changing with the Seasons

We are not the only ones to change our clothes with the seasons. We change our dress with the seasons to protect us from the weather. Animals do the same to protect themselves from the weather. They instinctively know when the weather will be changing.

For example, the arctic fox has a thick, white fur coat in the winter. It is not easy to see him in the snow. This helps him to hide from his enemies.

When spring comes, his white fur changes to brown. It is now the color of the ground.

One type of bird has white feathers in the winter. It, too, is hard to see in the snow. In the springtime, the bird molts. This means it sheds all of its feathers. The bird grows new feathers that are speckled. When the bird is very still, it looks like a rock.

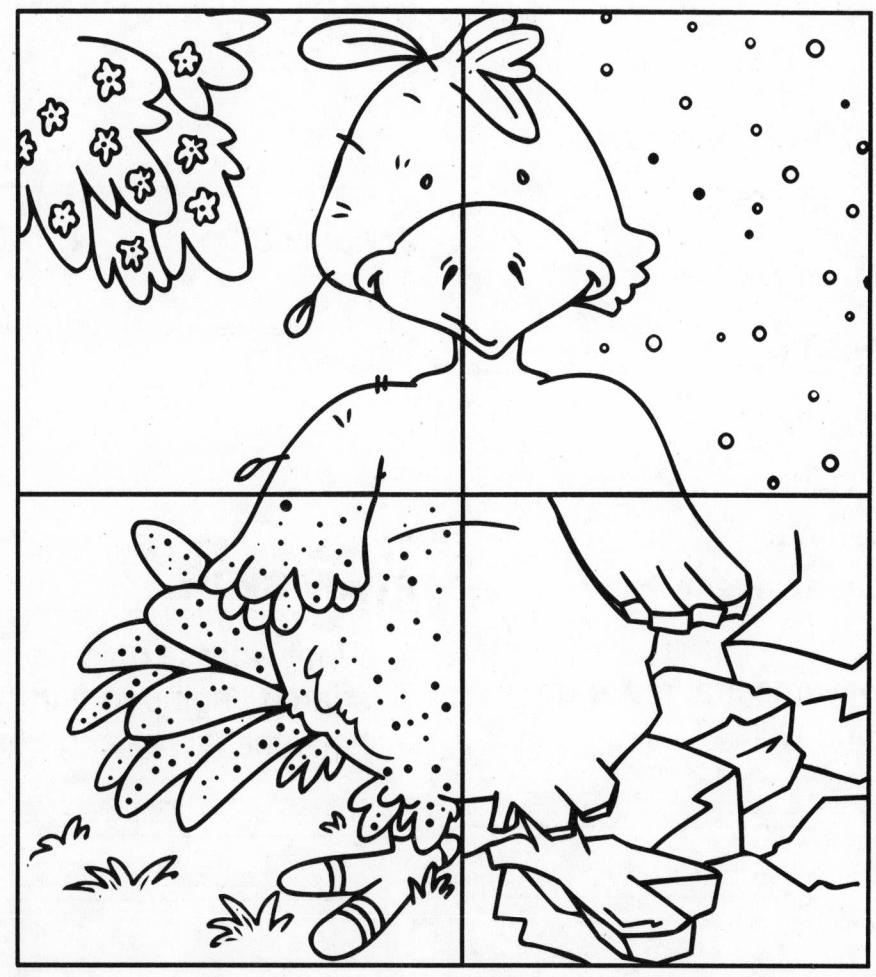

Reading Skills

1. What is this story mostly about?

   A. how people change

   B. how seasons change

   C. how animals change in seasons

2. What color is the arctic fox's fur in the winter?

   A. brown

   B. white

   C. black

3. What happens to the bird in the spring?

   A. It molts.

   B. It flies south.

   C. Its feathers turn red.

Vocabulary Skills

1. The word <u>molts</u> means

   A. to change colors.

   B. to shed feathers.

   C. to hide from an enemy.

2. Write the two words that make up each compound word.

   A. springtime _____ _____

   B. themselves _____ _____

   C. bluebird _____ _____

   D. wintertime _____ _____

Thinking Skills

Write these clothing words under the season you would most likely see them.

swimsuit   snow boots   jacket

sweater   coat   scarf

galoshes   raincoat   shorts

new school clothes   sandals

football jersey

1. winter   **3.** spring

_____   _____

_____   _____

_____   _____

2. summer   **4.** fall

_____   _____

_____   _____

_____   _____

Study Skills

1. What words could you type into a search engine to find out more about how animals change each season?

_____

_____

_____

Sing a song of summer,
my arms stretched open wide.
I run in the sunshine.
I play all day outside.

Hold on to the summer,
as long as you may.
Fall will come quickly
and shorten the day.

So play in the water,
roll in the grass.
It won't be long now,
before you'll be in class.

Reading Skills

1. What is the main idea?
   A.   Enjoy summer while it lasts.
   B.   Summer gets too hot.
   C.   School starts in the fall.

2. What season comes after summer?
   A.   winter
   B.   spring
   C.   fall

3. Put a √ by the things you can do in the summer.

   _____ play outside

   _____ rake leaves

   _____ go swimming

   _____ build a snowman

   _____ ride bikes

   _____ go to the park

Vocabulary Skills

Write the two little words that make up the **compound word**.

1. sunshine _____ _____

2. outside _____ _____

3. raindrop _____ _____

4. classroom _____ _____

Language Skills

A **noun** is a person, place, or thing. A **verb** shows action. Some words can be verbs or nouns depending on how they are used in the sentence. Read each sentence. Then write if the underlined word is a noun or a verb.

1. <u>Fall</u> is my favorite season. _____

2. The leaves <u>fall</u> from the tree. _____

3. Nick likes to <u>play</u> football. _____

4. My sister went to see a <u>play</u> _____

5. I <u>roll</u> in the grass. _____

6. I had a <u>roll</u> with my soup. _____

Thinking Skills

Write each word under its season.

football	sledding	snow
leaves falling	flowers	swimming
school starts	hot weather	shorts
mittens	baby animals	rain

1. winter   2. spring

   _____   _____

   _____   _____

   _____   _____

3. summer   4. fall

   _____   _____

   _____   _____

   _____   _____

Lemonade

Lemonade for sale!
Lemonade for sale!

The sun is hot.
It'll hit the spot.

We made it sweet.
It's quite a treat.

We've got lots of ice,
It's really quite nice.

It's just one dime.
You've got the time.

Try our delicious lemonade—
It's simply the best we've ever made.

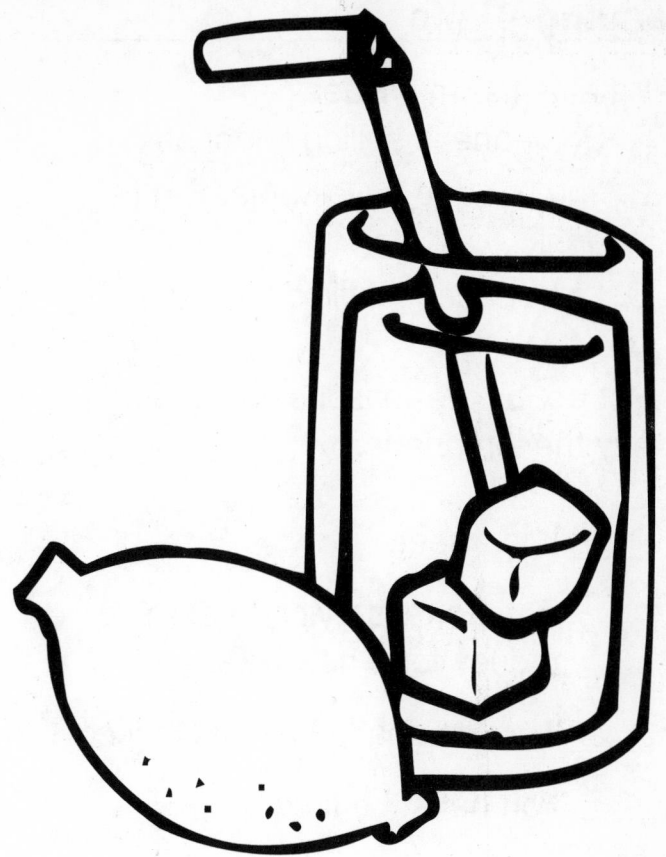

www.summerbridgeactivities.com

Reading Skills

1. What is the main idea?
   A. Someone is selling lemonade.
   B. You need to have something to drink.
   C. Lemonade is delicious.

2. Put a √ by the reasons you should buy the lemonade.

_____ It is sweet.

_____ Someone is trying to earn money for a new bike.

_____ The lemonade has lots of ice.

_____ You have the time.

_____ You don't have any lemonade.

Language Skills

Write the two words that make up each **contraction**.

1. it'll   _____ _____

2. it's   _____ _____

3. you've   _____ _____

4. I've   _____ _____

5. we've   _____ _____

Vocabulary Skills

1. What does "It will hit the spot" mean?
   A. The lemonade is just what you need when it's hot.
   B. The lemonade will spill on the right spot.
   C. The lemonade has spots in it.

2. What does "It's quite a treat" mean?
   A. The lemonade is really sweet.
   B. The lemonade is a special surprise.
   C. You should drink lemonade on Halloween.

Thinking Skills

1. Draw a poster selling something you like to eat.

Let's Go Shopping

"Let's go shopping," my mom said. "What do we need?" asked my dad.

"How about a dish for our fish?" I suggested. "But we don't have a fish," said my dad.

"How about a wig for our pig?" suggested my little brother. "But we don't have a pig," said my dad.

"How about a hat for our cat?" suggested my big sister. "But we don't have a cat," said my dad.

"How about a log for our dog?" suggested Mom. "We don't have a dog," said my dad.

"It seems to me," said my mom, "that what we need is a pet."

So we went shopping for a pet.

puppies

kittens

fish

www.summerbridgeactivities.com

Reading Skills

1. What did the family decide they needed?
   A. a dish for a fish
   B. nothing
   C. a pet

2. Write the person who said each sentence.
   A. Who said, "How about a hat for our cat?" _____

   B. Who said, "What we need is a pet"? _____

   C. Who said, "But we don't have a fish"? _____

   D. Who said, "How about a wig for our pig?" _____

Vocabulary Skills

1. Draw a line between the rhyming words.

   dish   cat

   wig   dog

   hat   fish

   log   pig

Language Skills

Quotation marks are used to show the words that someone says. Put quotation marks around what is being said in each sentence.

1. Let's go shopping, said Mother.

2. Can we buy a pet? asked my brother.

3. We don't need a pet, said my father.

4. That dog needs a home, said my mother.

5. Okay, said my father, we can buy the dog.

Study Skills

A **want ad** is an advertisement in a newspaper or magazine. Use the want ad to answer the questions.

FOR SALE
A purebred collie. $50.00 to a good home. Call Sam at 446-2111

---

1. What is for sale? _____

2. Who should you call if you want to buy the dog? _____

3. How much does the dog cost? _____

4. What number should you call if you want to buy the dog? _____

My Cat

Have you seen my cat?
    Yes, I've seen your cat.

Really? My cat is big.
    I saw a big cat.

My cat has spots.
    I saw a big cat with spots.

My cat's spots are black.
    I saw a big cat with black spots.

My cat runs fast.
    I saw a big cat with black
    spots running fast.

You did see my cat!
Where is it?
    I don't know.
    I saw it last week.

www.summerbridgeactivities.com

Reading Skills

1. What was the writer looking for?

   _____

2. What does the cat look like?

   _____

3. Why didn't the person know where

   the cat was? _____

   _____

Vocabulary Skills

1. Draw a line between the opposites.

big	black
stripes	slow
white	spots
fast	little

Thinking Skills

1. Why didn't the person in the story find
   the cat?

   _____

   _____

   _____

Language Skills

Circle the correct short vowel.

1. My cat has sp__ts, not stripes.
   a or o

2. My cat is b__g, not small.
   a or i

3. My cat runs f__st, not slow.
   a or i

4. My cat is bl__ck, not white.
   a or o

Study Skills

Read the poster. Answer the questions.

LOST CAT
Big, black cat with spots.
Please call Rachel 448-8888
REWARD

1. What is this poster about? _____

2. Whom should you call if you find the

   cat? _____

3. What number should you call?

   _____

4. What is a "reward"? _____

I wonder if animals have dreams.

Does a fish dream of swimming in the sky?
Does a bird dream of flying in the ocean?

I wonder if monkeys dream of learning in
school, while children dream of swinging
from vines.

Or maybe worms dream of being as big as snakes,
and snakes dream of having legs like a centipede.

I wonder.

Reading Skills

Write **T** if the sentence is true. Write **F** if the sentence is false.

1. _____ Fish swim in the sky.

2. _____ Monkeys swing from vines.

3. _____ Snakes have legs like centipedes.

4. _____ Birds fly in the sky.

5. What does the author wonder about?
A. if monkeys wish they could go to school
B. if animals have dreams
C. if animals are happy

Language Skills

Write the **base word** on the line.

1. swimming _____

2. flying _____

3. learning _____

4. swinging _____

5. being _____

6. having _____

Thinking Skills

1. Do you think animals have dreams? Tell why or why not.

_____

_____

_____

_____

_____

_____

_____

Study Skills

Use the encyclopedias below. Write the number of the volume where you would find information on each animal below.

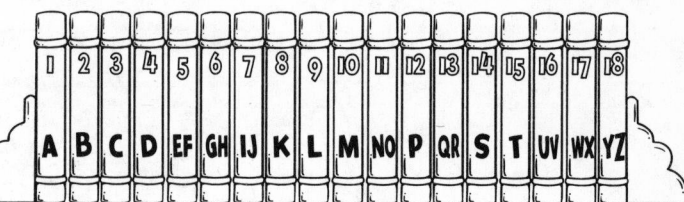

1. fish _____

2. birds _____

3. monkeys _____

4. worms _____

5. snakes _____

6. centipedes _____

Reading Connection—Grade 2—RBP3810   www.summerbridgeactivities.com   ©RBP Books

The Swamp

In the jungle there was a swamp.

Five wild pigs tromped by. "It's hot!" they squealed. So into the swamp they went.

Four monkeys came swinging by. "It's hot," they chattered. So into the swamp they went.

Three frogs hopped by. "It's hot," they croaked. So into the swamp they went.

Two snakes slithered by. "It's hot," they hissed. So into the swamp they went.

One big alligator wriggled by. "It's not hot," he grinned, showing his great big teeth, "but I am hungry." So into the swamp he went.

Suddenly out from the swamp came two snakes, three frogs, four monkeys, and five wild pigs. It didn't feel so hot anymore.

www.summerbridgeactivities.com

Reading Connection—Grade 2—RBP3810

Reading Skills

1. Why did the animals get out of the swamp?

   A. They weren't hot anymore.

   B. It was too crowded.

   C. So the alligator wouldn't eat them.

2. Number the sentences in the order that they happened.

   _____ Three frogs hopped by.

   _____ Four monkeys came swinging by.

   _____ Two snakes slithered by.

   _____ Five wild pigs tromped by.

   _____ One big alligator wriggled by.

Vocabulary Skills

Synonyms are words that mean the same or almost the same thing. Cross out the word in each group that is not a synonym of the other words.

1. said   yelled

   asked   kicked

2. jump   roll

   hop   leap

3. cried   laughed

   giggled   chuckled

4. moan   clap

   groan   sigh

Language Skills

Write the **base word** on the line.

1. tromped _____

2. swinging_____

3. hopped_____

4. slithered_____

5. grinned_____

Study Skills

At the top of each page in a dictionary are **guide words**. The guide word on the *left* tells you the first word found on the page. The guide word on the *right* tells you the last word on the page. Circle the word that would be found on the page with the following guide words.

1. **patter—penguin**

   panda   pig   paw

2. **match—monkey**

   moan   magic   motor

3. **alligator—anteater**

   antelope   animal   antler

4. **bear—buffalo**

   bunny   bat   bison

My dog, Eli, loves to go to the river. Every Saturday morning I take Eli to the park by the river to play. The first thing Eli does when we get there is run down to the water.

Eli likes to take a drink and splash around. The cold water doesn't bother him. When he gets out of the water, he shakes and shakes. I stand back so all the water doesn't get on me. Then he looks for a rock in the sun to take a nap on. He sleeps there until I whistle for him that it is time to go home.

I think our Saturday trips to the river are something that Eli looks forward to all week.

Reading Skills

1. What is the main idea?
   A. Eli takes a nap.
   B. Eli loves the river.
   C. Eli is a good dog.

2. Number the sentences in the order that they happened in the story.

   _____ I whistle for Eli when it is time to go home.

   _____ Eli runs to the water.

   _____ Eli takes a nap.

   _____ Eli splashes in the water.

3. What does Eli do when he gets out of the water?
   A. rolls in the dirt
   B. shakes and shakes
   C. licks his fur

Vocabulary Skills

Choose the correct short vowel.

1. I have a d ___ g.
   i or o

2. Eli likes to dr ___ nk the water.
   a or i

3. Eli n ___ ps on a rock.
   i or a

4. Eli finds a rock in the s ___ n.
   u or a

Language Skills

Sometimes the same word can be used as a noun or as a verb. Write **noun** or **verb** to tell how each underlined word is used in each sentence.

1. Can I have a drink, please? _____

2. My dogs drink a lot of water. _____

3. My dog made a big splash in the water. _____

4. The children splash in the water. _____

5. I order a shake with my hamburger.
   _____

6. My hands shake when I am nervous.
   _____

Study Skills

Words in a dictionary are organized alphabetically. Number the words below in **alphabetical order**.

1. ____splash
   ____stand
   ____shake
   ____sleep

3. ____ love
   ____ look
   ____ lake
   ____ lamp

2. ____thing
   ____take
   ____think
   ____then

4. ____ whistle
   ____ water
   ____ winter
   ____ weather

My brother Juan made a birdhouse. The birdhouse was beautiful. I hung it in the front yard. The neighbors asked about our new birdhouse. This gave me an idea. Juan and I could earn money selling birdhouses.

Juan built three more birdhouses. I made posters. I put them around the neighborhood. We charged four dollars for each birdhouse. We sold all three birdhouses the first day. Five other neighbors asked for birdhouses, too.

With my brains and my brother's birdhouses, we started our own business.

www.summerbridgeactivities.com

Reading Skills

1. What is the main idea?

   A. Everybody loves birdhouses.

   B. starting a birdhouse business

   C. how to put your brother to work

2. Who is writing this story?

   A. Juan's mother

   B. Juan's friend

   C. Juan's sister

3. Put a √ by the ways Juan's sister used her brains.

   _____ She got the idea to sell the birdhouses.

   _____ She painted the birdhouses.

   _____ She made posters.

   _____ She made five more birdhouses.

   _____ She hung the posters around the neighborhood.

4. Number these sentences in the order they happened in the story.

   _____ More neighbors asked for birdhouses.

   _____ Juan built a birdhouse.

   _____ Juan's sister made posters.

   _____ Juan and his sister sold three birdhouses.

   _____ Juan built more birdhouses.

Vocabulary Skills

1. Draw a line from the **present tense** verb to its correct **past tense**.

make	built
hang	gave
give	sold
build	made
sell	hung

Study Skills

Divide the following words into **syllables**. Use a dictionary if you need help.

bird • house

1. birdhouse_____

2. beautiful_____

3. poster_____

4. dollar _____

5. business_____

The Birds in My Garden

I like to watch the birds in my garden. The robins come as the snow is melting. The male robin has a red breast. He helped his mate build a nest in the cherry tree. I peeked into the nest. I counted three tiny eggs.

Two magpies live in my garden. Their feathers are shiny black and white. The magpies built their huge nest in the pine tree. Magpies can copy the sounds of other birds. They are noisy and sometimes quarrel.

My favorite birds to watch are quail. They have a topknot on their head that bobs when they walk. Quail make their nests on the ground under a bush. They live in families called flocks. They can run very fast. When they are frightened, they scatter to different places. When the danger is gone, they whistle to each other to come back. I love watching the baby quail follow their parents. Sometimes, I see them in the road, and I worry they might get hit by a car. They seem to always scatter just in time.

www.summerbridgeactivities.com

Reading Skills

1. What does the child in this story like to do?

    A. watch birds

    B. collect birds

    C. watch animals

2. Which bird is <u>not</u> in the garden?

    A. magpie

    B. lark

    C. robin

    D. quail

3. Draw a line between each bird and where it builds its nest.

    A.   robin   under a bush

    B.   magpie   in a pine tree

    C.   quail   in a cherry tree

Vocabulary Skills

1. What does the word <u>flock</u> mean?

    A. a group of birds

    B. a family

    C. a group of animals

Language Skills

Write the **base word** for the following words:

1. peeked _____

2. counted _____

3. families _____

4. watching _____

5. places _____

Study Skills

Complete the following outline.

I. Robins

    1. come early in spring

    2. males have a red breast

    3. _____

II. Magpies

    1. _____

    2. build nests in pine trees

    3. copy sounds

    4. _____

III. Quail

    1. have a topknot

    2. _____

    3. run fast

Animals move in different ways. Some animals move on four legs. Horses gallop on four legs. Dogs run on four legs. Lions pounce on four legs.

Some animals move on two legs. Kangaroos hop on two legs. Ducks waddle on two legs.

Some animals move through water. Some animals move in the sky. Other animals move on the ground. Fish swim in the water. Birds fly in the sky. Snakes slither along the ground.

It's fun to think about all the different ways animals move.

www.summerbridgeactivities.com **Reading Connection—Grade 2—RBP3810**

Reading Skills

1. What is the main idea?

   A. Ducks waddle.

   B. Animals move in different ways.

   C. Animals are different in many ways.

2. Draw a line from the animal to how it moves.

   horse   fly

   kangaroo   swims

   duck   slithers

   fish   gallops

   birds   waddles

   snake   hops

Vocabulary Skills

Circle the correct vowel.

1. Dogs r __ n.
   o or u

2. Kangaroos h __ p.
   o or u

3. Fish sw __ m.
   i or o

4. Snakes sl __ ther.
   i or o

Thinking Skills

1. Put each animal in the correct group. Some animals may go in more than one group.

   cat   whale

   chicken   goldfish

   robin   deer

   owl   penguin

   <u>Moves on two feet</u>

   _____

   _____

   <u>Moves on four feet</u>

   _____

   _____

   <u>Flies</u>

   _____

   _____

   <u>Swims</u>

   _____

   _____

Insects

There are about a million different types of insects. Insects come in many different shapes and sizes, but all insects have some things in common.

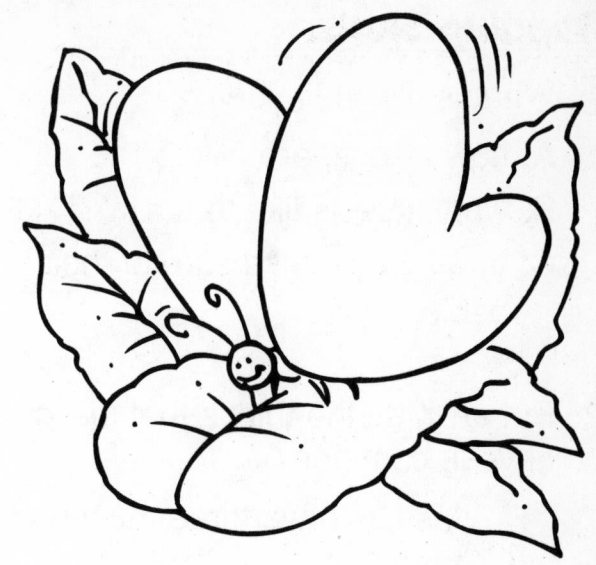

All insects have three main body parts. They have a head, a body that is called a <u>thorax</u>, and an abdomen. All insects have six legs. Most insects have two feelers on their heads called antennae. Many insects use their antennae to see, taste, and hear. All insects hatch from eggs.

Reading Skills

1. What is the main idea?

   A. how insects are alike

   B. what insects like to eat

   C. how insects take care of their babies

2. Put an **X** by the things that insects have in common.

   _____ Insects have three main body parts.

   _____ Insects have six legs.

   _____ Insects and bugs are different.

   _____ Insects have feelers on their heads.

   _____ Insects are pests.

Vocabulary Skills

Match the word with the correct meaning. Write the letter on the line.

1. _____ head

2. _____ thorax

3. _____ abdomen

4. _____ antennae

A. the bottom part of the insect's body

B. the top part of the insect's body

C. the middle part of the insect's body

D. feelers on the insect's head

Language Skills

Circle the correct vowel.

1. Insects can be many different sh __ pes.
   a or i

2. Insects can be many different s __ zes.
   a or i

3. Insects use their antennae to t __ ste.
   a or o

Study Skills

The **title page** of a book gives you important information. Use this title page to answer the questions below.

> **The Interesting World of Insects**
>
> Joshua Ryan
>
> Rainbow Bridge Publishing
> Salt Lake City, Utah

1. What is the title of the book?

   _____

2. Who is the author? _____

3. Who published the book?

   _____

4. Where was the book published?

   _____

The Ladybug

The ladybug is sometimes called a ladybird. It is a very interesting insect. Most ladybugs are red or yellow with black spots. The California ladybug's shell is yellow with black spots. This beetle has a tiny head and no neck. Its body is round and shaped like half a pea. It can run very fast on its short legs. The ladybug's wings are tucked under its shell. It can fly very well.

The ladybug lays its eggs on the underside of green leaves. When the grubs hatch, they are very hungry. They quickly start to eat plant lice. Lice can ruin a farmer's crop. Fruit growers like ladybugs because they eat harmful lice.

The California ladybug was brought to the United States from Australia. It helps protect orange, lemon, and grapefruit trees.

Reading Skills

1. What is <u>not</u> true about ladybugs?

   A. They have small heads.

   B. They have no neck.

   C. They can't fly.

2. Where does the ladybug lay its eggs?

   A. in a nest

   B. under a leaf

   C. on the bark of a tree

3. What type of animal is a ladybug?

   A. an insect

   B. a bird

   C. can't tell from the story

4. What do grubs eat?

   A. leaves

   B. fruit

   C. lice

Vocabulary Skills

1. What is another name for the ladybug?

   A. the love bug

   B. ladybird

   C. birdbug

2. In this story a grub is _____.

   A. something to eat

   B. a baby ladybug

   C. a leaf

Language Skills

1. **Proper nouns** are specific names of persons, places, or things. Proper nouns always begin with a capital letter. Find three proper nouns in the last paragraph.

   _____

   _____

   _____

Study Skills

1. Words in an **index** are listed alphabetically. Number these words as they would appear in the index of a book about ladybugs.

   _____ larva

   _____ beetles

   _____ lice

   _____ grub

   _____ insects

   _____ eggs

   _____ wings

Ants

Ants can be found almost anywhere on our planet. There are about 20,000 different types of ants. Ants are amazing insects. An ant can carry things almost twice its own size. Ants use feelers on top of their heads to find food.

Many ants have very sharp teeth. An ant's jaw opens sideways. Ants use their jaws to eat. They also use their jaws to carry their babies and to fight. Ants are social insects. They live in large groups called <u>colonies</u>.

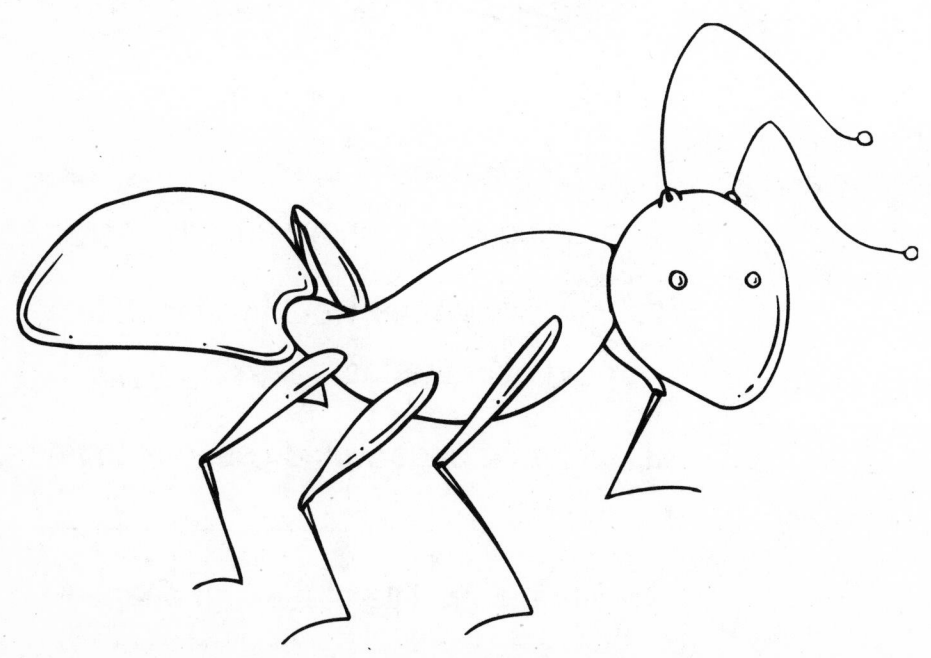

Reading Skills

1. What is the main idea?

A. Ants are strong.

B. Ants are amazing.

C. Ants have big jaws.

2. Put a √ by the sentences that give details about the main idea.

_____ An ant can carry things twice its size.

_____ Ants use feelers to help them find food.

_____ I have an ant farm.

_____ An ant's jaw opens sideways.

_____ Some ants were in the cupboard.

Language Skills

Words like _they_ and _it_ take the place of other words. Write the words _they_ and _it_ stand for in each sentence.

1. An ant is very strong. _It_ can carry things twice its size.

_It_ stands for _____.

2. Ants have big jaws. _They_ use their jaws to eat.

They stands for _____.

Vocabulary Skills

1. What does _amazing_ mean?

A. interesting

B. able to go through a maze

C. small

Study Skills

Use the table of contents to answer the questions.

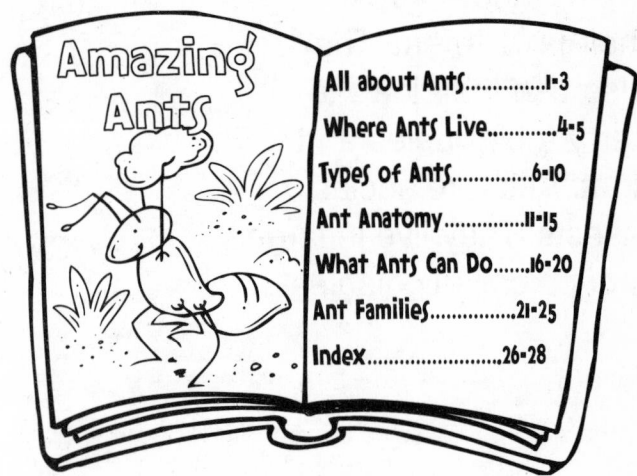

1. On what page could you begin reading about where ants live? _____

2. In what chapter would you look to read about ant families? _____

3. On what page would you look to find the index? _____

4. What is the title of the first chapter?

_____

The Koala

Koalas live in Australia. They spend most of their time high up in tall eucalyptus trees. Koalas eat the leaves from the tree. They eat about two to three pounds of leaves every day. They drink very little water. The eucalyptus leaves give the koala the water it needs.

Many people think koalas are bears because they look like bear cubs. Koalas are not bears. They are <u>marsupials</u>. Marsupials are a special kind of mammal. They have pouches where their babies go to stay warm and safe. Koalas have pouches just like another animal that begins with a K. Can you guess what it is? The kangaroo.

www.summerbridgeactivities.com   **Reading Connection—Grade 2—RBP3810**

Reading Skills

1. What is the story about?

   A. Australia

   B. koalas

   C. eucalyptus trees

2. Where do koalas spend most of their time?

   A. in eucalyptus trees

   B. in their mothers' pouches

   C. in caves with bears

3. How would you describe this story?

   A. silly

   B. true

   C. make-believe

Vocabulary Skills

1. What is a marsupial?

   A. a mammal with a pouch

   B. an animal that swims underwater

   C. a mammal with a long trunk

2. What is a eucalyptus?

   A. a type of marsupial

   B. a type of tree

   C. a baby koala

Language Skills

Write the **plural** of each word.

1. koala _____

2. marsupial _____

3. pouch _____

4. baby _____

5. bear _____

6. leaf _____

Study Skills

1. Using information from the reading, write three words that you could type into a search engine to find out more information about koalas on the Internet.

   _____

   _____

   _____

2. Use a dictionary or encyclopedia to find another marsupial that is not a koala or a kangaroo. Write it below.

   _____

Bats

Many people are afraid of bats, but bats are not harmful. They can be helpful. Bats help by eating insects and other pests. There really is no reason to be afraid of bats.

There are many myths about bats. A <u>myth</u> is something that some people believe, but it is not true. One myth is that a bat will fly into your hair and get stuck. The truth is, bats are afraid of people. The last place a bat wants to be is in your hair. Another myth is that bats suck people's blood. The truth is, most bats don't like blood. They eat insects or fruit.

Even though bats are not harmful, they are wild animals. It is not a good idea to try to catch a bat. Even the most helpful animals will bite if they are scared. If you see a bat, don't be afraid. But just look, don't touch.

Reading Skills

1. What is the main idea?

   A. Bats are scary.

   B. Bats make good pets.

   C. Bats aren't harmful.

2. Write **T** if the sentence is true. Write **F** if the sentence is false.

   _____ Bats eat insects.

   _____ Bats fly into people's hair.

   _____ Bats suck people's blood.

   _____ Bats are wild animals.

Vocabulary Skills

1. Draw a line between the opposites.

harmful	tame
truth	helpful
afraid	myth
wild	brave

2. What is a <u>myth</u>?

   A. something people believe that is not true

   B. something people eat but do not like

   C. something people do for fun

Language Skills

Is and **are** are verbs. Use <u>is</u> when the subject is one. Use <u>are</u> when the subject is two or more. Write <u>is</u> or <u>are</u> on the line to make the sentence correct.

1. The bat _____ a helpful animal.

2. Bats _____ afraid of people.

3. Some people _____ afraid of bats.

4. A bat _____ a wild animal.

5. Insects _____ a food for bats.

Study Skills

Complete the following outline.

I. How bats are helpful

   A. Bats eat insects.

   B. Bats eat _____.

II. Myths about bats

   A. Bats fly into people's _____.

   B. Bats _____.

Thinking Skills

1. Why do you think some people are afraid of bats?

   _____

   _____

   _____

Germs

Germs are things you do not want to share. Germs can make you sick. Even though you cannot see germs, they get into the body in lots of ways. Germs get in the body through the nose, mouth, eyes, and cuts in the skin. We share germs when we sneeze or cough and do not cover our mouths. We share germs when we drink from the same cup or eat off the same plate.

To keep germs to yourself and to get well:
- Wash your hands with soap.
- Cover your mouth when you cough or sneeze.
- Do not share food or drink.
- Keep your fingers out of your nose and mouth.
- Do not rub your eyes.
- Get lots of sunshine and fresh air.
- Eat healthy meals.
- Get plenty of sleep.

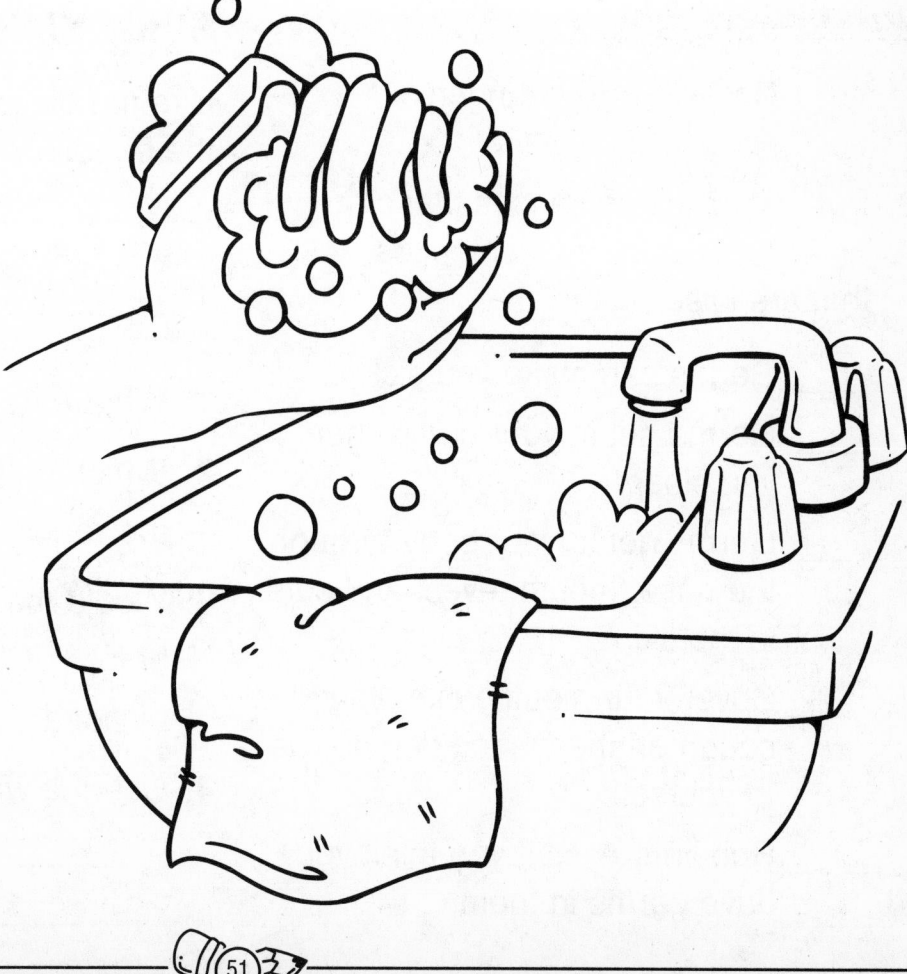

Reading Skills

1. What is the main idea?
   A. Germs are things you do not want to share.
   B. You can't see germs.
   C. Wash your hands often.

2. Put a √ by the ways you can keep germs to yourself.

   _____ Wash your hands with soap.

   _____ Stay away from animals.

   _____ Cover your mouth when you cough or sneeze.

   _____ Eat dessert three times a week.

   _____ Get plenty of sleep.

   _____ Eat healthy meals.

   _____ Never talk to strangers.

3. Put a **T** by the sentences that are true. Put an **F** by the sentences that are false.

   _____ Germs can make you sick.

   _____ Germs get in your body when you sleep.

   _____ Germs get in your body through the nose, mouth, eyes, and cuts in the skin.

   _____ Cover your mouth when you cough or sneeze to keep germs to yourself.

   _____ Rub your eyes if you think you have germs in them.

Language Skills

Choose the correct short vowel.

1. Germs can make you s ___ ck.
   i or o

2. Germs get in the body through c ___ ts in your skin.
   a or u

3. Do not r ___ b your eyes.
   o or u

4. Get l ___ ts of sunshine.
   i or o

Study Skills

Use the dictionary entry below to answer the questions.

germ (jûrm), n. 1. disease-producing microbe. 2. a bud or seed.

1. What part of speech is <u>germ</u>? _____

2. Which definition of <u>germ</u> is used in the reading? _____

3. Would the word <u>germinate</u> come before or after the word germ in the dictionary? _____

4. Use the word <u>germ</u> in a sentence

   _____

   _____

Stamp Collecting

So you want to be a <u>philatelist</u>? If you collect stamps, that's what you are! Stamp collecting is an old hobby that is fun and interesting.

If you want to start collecting stamps, you will need a few supplies. You can find these supplies at your local hobby shop. You will need a pair of tweezers. Use tweezers when you handle the stamps so that you do not get the stamps dirty. You will also need an album with plastic pages.

You start by collecting some stamps. The stamps you collect may be new or used. You can collect stamps from letters that arrive at your house. You can also buy special stamps to add to your collection.

Next, decide how to organize your stamps. You can organize them by their value, by the place they are from, or by a theme.

You will want to keep your stamp albums in a cool, dry place away from direct sunlight. Heat, sun, and damp-ness can ruin your stamps.

Reading Skills

1. What is the main idea?

_____ Stamp collecting is a fun and interesting hobby.

_____ You can organize stamps in many different ways.

_____ Stamps come from all over the world.

2. Put a √ by things that you need to start a stamp collection.

_____ stamps

_____ an album

_____ a dictionary

_____ tweezers

_____ plastic pages

_____ rubber gloves

Language Skills

Write the **base word** for each of the following words.

1. collection _____

2. supplies _____

3. organization _____

4. dampness _____

Vocabulary Skills

1. What is a philatelist? _____

Draw a line between the item you need for stamp collecting and its use.

2. tweezers   to protect the stamps

3. plastic pages   to handle the stamps

4. albums   to keep the albums safe from heat, sun, and dampness

5. cool, dry place   to organize the pages

Study Skills

Complete the following outline.

I. Stamp Collecting Supplies

A. _____

B. _____

C. _____

II. Collecting Stamps

A. _____

B. _____

III. Organizing Stamps

A. _____

B. _____

C. _____

Scrapbooking

Scrapbooking has been around for a long time. But in the last few years it has become a popular hobby. What used to be a simple way of storing pictures and memories has become an art. Businesses have been started to sell scrapbooking supplies. They sell special paper, special stickers and cut outs, special letters, and special albums. They also sell books about how to make scrapbooks.

Scrapbooking is different from organizing photograph albums. Photograph albums have only pictures to tell the story. Scrapbooks include lots of writing and mementos to preserve the memories.

One way to start scrapbooking is to choose a theme. The theme may be sports or school or a vacation. Once you decide on your theme, look through the pictures and mementos that you have. Select the ones that best tell the story that you want to remember. Then choose the paper you will use. Lay the pictures out on the pages. Think of a headline for the page. Write something about each picture. Be sure to include the names of the people in each picture and the date. Everyone thinks they will remember, but they don't. Time has a way of erasing the memories. That is why scrapbooks are such a nice way to preserve those memories.

Reading Skills

1. Scrapbooking supplies include

    A. pieces of scrap metal.

    B. special paper, photographs, stickers and cut outs, letters, and albums.

    C. pictures and albums.

2. Which of the following would probably not be a theme for a scrapbook?

    A. school events

    B. a special vacation

    C. lunch in the cafeteria

3. "Time has a way of erasing the memories" means what?

    A. Over time we forget.

    B. Time keeps ticking away.

    C. Our clocks take over our minds.

Vocabulary Skills

Write the two words that make up each **compound word**.

1. scrapbook _____ _____

2. headline _____ _____

3. something _____ _____

4. everyone _____ _____

5. bookstore _____ _____

6. In the story, the word <u>preserve</u> means

    A. to make jam.

    B. to save.

    C. a forest.

7. Find three words in the story that have the word part **mem** that means to "bring to mind."

_____

_____

_____

Language Skills

Write the **base word**.

1. storing _____

2. memories _____

3. supplies _____

4. organizing _____

5. writing _____

6. erasing _____

Reading Connection—Grade 2—RBP3810   www.summerbridgeactivities.com   ©RBP Books

Mercer Mayer

Mercer Mayer's books can be found in every library and bookstore. Mr. Mayer's name is on more than 300 books. He has both written and illustrated books. Some of his most popular books include *There's a Nightmare in My Closet, Liz Lou and the Great Yeller Belly Swamp, Just for You,* and *A Boy, a Dog, and a Frog.* Mr. Mayer likes to write about things that happened to him as a child.

Mercer Mayer was born on December 30, 1943. He was born in Arkansas. His father was in the navy, so his family lived in many different places. When he was 13 he moved to Hawaii. After high school, he went to school to study art. Then he worked for an advertising company in New York. He published his first book in 1967. He and his wife work together on the Little Critter stories. He has two children. Now he works from his home in Connecticut.

www.summerbridgeactivities.com

Reading Skills

Write **T** before the statements that are true. Write **F** before the statements that are false.

1. _____ Mercer Mayer is a character in a book.

2. _____ Mercer Mayer likes to write about things he did as a child.

3. _____ Mercer Mayer lived in many different places.

4. _____ Mercer Mayer never got married.

Vocabulary Skills

Circle the correct answer.

1. This narrative is called a <u>biography</u>. Based on what you read, what do you think a biography is?

   A. a story made up about a character from a book

   B. a true story that tells about the life of a real person

   C. a short, funny story

2. What is another word for <u>illustrated</u>?

   A. described

   B. drew

   C. wrote

Language Skills

Commas are used to separate words in a series or in a date. Place the commas correctly in the sentences below.

1. My brother was born November 15 2001.

2. I like to eat pizza popcorn pretzels and pickles.

3. My favorite Mercer Mayer books are *There's a Nightmare in My Closet There's an Alligator under My Bed* and *Terrible Troll.*

4. The title of the book is *A Boy a Dog and a Frog.*

5. Mercer Mayer's birthday is December 30 1943.

Study Skills

Mercer Mayer lived in many different places. Use the encyclopedias below. Write the number of the volume where you would find information on each of the following places.

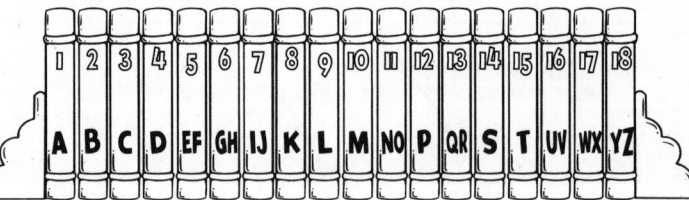

1. Arkansas _____

2. Hawaii _____

3. New York _____

4. Connecticut _____

Sammy Sosa

Sammy Sosa is one of the greatest baseball players ever. He was born November 12, 1968, in the Dominican Republic. While he was growing up, Sammy's family was very poor. He could not afford a glove, bat, or ball. So Sammy used a rolled-up sock as a baseball, a stick as a bat, milk cartons for gloves, and cardboard for bases. Today, Sammy is one of the highest paid baseball players. He plays right field for the Chicago Cubs. He joined the Cubs team in 1992.

In 1998, Sammy Sosa made baseball history. He broke the record for the most home runs hit during a season. That same year, Sammy was named baseball's Most Valuable Player (MVP). The next year, Sammy again made history by becoming the only player to hit 60 home runs in two seasons. On April 6, 2003, Sammy became the eighteenth player to hit 500 home runs.

© RBP Books　　www.summerbridgeactivities.com　　Reading Connection—Grade 2—RBP3810

Reading Skills

1. Check the sentence that best states the main idea of this biography.

   _____ Sammy is one of the highest paid baseball players.

   _____ Sammy is one of the greatest baseball players.

   _____ Sammy plays right field for the Chicago Cubs.

2. Check the phrase that tells what Sammy Sosa is best known for.

   _____ playing baseball

   _____ growing up poor

   _____ being born in the Dominican Republic

3. Write **T** by the sentences that are true. Write **F** by the sentences that are false.

   _____ Sammy was born in Chicago.

   _____ In 1968, Sammy was named baseball's MVP.

   _____ Sammy has hit at least 500 home runs.

   _____ Sammy plays for the Chicago Cubs.

   _____ While he was growing up, Sammy's family was very poor.

Language Skills

Write the two words that make up each **compound word** below.

1. baseball   _____ _____

2. cardboard   _____ _____

Write the **base word** for the words below.

3. greatest _____

4. growing _____

5. rolled _____

6. highest _____

7. valuable _____

Vocabulary Skills

Match the words with their meanings as used in this biography.

1. MVP   _____ **A.** able to buy

2. afford   _____ **B.** the best accomplishment

3. season   _____ **C.** record of events

4. history   _____ **D.** period of time

5. record   _____ **E.** most valuable player

Study Skills

Look at the timeline. Write the letter beside the event that happened in Sammy Sosa's life.

Timeline of Sammy Sosa's Life

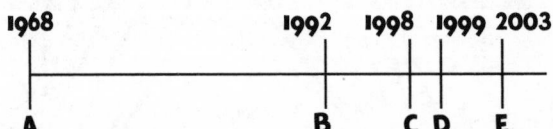

1. _____ Sammy broke the record for the most home runs in a season.

2. _____ Sammy was born in the Dominican Republic.

3. _____ Sammy hit his 500th home run.

4. _____ Sammy became the only player to hit 60 home runs in two seasons.

5. _____ Sammy joined the Chicago Cubs.

Two living things, blowing in the wind.
One stands straight, the other bends.

One is a strong tree growing tall.
The other is grass ever so small.

Both are Mother Nature's gift.
The tree you can climb. On the grass you can sit.

Green is their color, brought on by the spring.
Grass or trees, they both make me sing!

Reading Skills

1. What two things is the poem compar-ing?

   A. grass and tree

   B. tree and flower

   C. wind and rain

2. How does the writer feel about grass and trees?

   _____

   _____

Thinking Skills

1. Think about how grass and trees are alike and how they are different. Put an **X** in the column the words describe.

Alike or Different?	grass	tree
living thing		
stands straight in the wind		
bends in the wind		
tall		
small		
Mother Nature's gift		
you can climb it		
you can sit on it		
green in color		

Vocabulary Skills

Draw a line between the rhyming words in the three columns.

1. tall   lift   wall

2. gift   sing   thing

3. spring   small   sift

Write an **opposite** for each word.

4. straight _____

5. tall _____

6. stand _____

Study Skills

Study the diagram and answer the questions.

1. What are the flowers on a tree called? _____

2. What is the bump on the trunk of a tree called? _____

3. What part of the tree is below the ground? _____

4. From what part of the tree do the leaves grow? _____

Reading Connection—Grade 2—RBP3810   www.summerbridgeactivities.com   ©RBP Books

Did you know there are two kinds of twins? Chris and Will are twins. They were born on December 22 and have the same parents. Some twins look alike. They are called identical twins. Chris and Will are not identical twins. Chris and Will are <u>fraternal</u> <u>twins</u>. Fraternal twins do not always look alike. In fact, Will has curly red hair, but Chris has straight brown hair. Chris's eyes are green, and Will's eyes are blue.

All twins are alike in some ways and different in other ways. For example, Chris and Will are both in the second grade. But Chris is in Miss Blinn's class, and Will is in Mrs. Thornton's class. Both boys are good at reading. But Chris is a good artist, and Will is a good ballplayer.

Reading Skills

1. What is the main idea?

   A. Chris and Will are fraternal twins.

   B. Chris and Will have different teachers.

   C. Chris and Will look different.

2. Chris and Will are

   A. cousins

   B. fraternal twins

   C. identical twins

3. What are the two types of twins?

   A. fraternal and maternal

   B. fraternal and identical

   C. Chris and Will

Thinking Skills

Think about how the boys are alike and how they are different. Put an **X** in the column of the boy the words describe.

Alike or Different?	Chris	Will
1. born on December 22		
2. curly red hair and blue eyes		
3. straight brown hair and green eyes		
4. in the second grade		
5. in Miss Blinn's class		
6. good at reading		
7. a good artist		
8. a good ballplayer		

Vocabulary Skills

1. Finish the sentence: Identical twins…

   A. look alike.

   B. like the same things.

   C. don't look alike.

2. Finish the sentence: Fraternal twins…

   A. look alike.

   B. don't like the same things.

   C. don't always look alike.

Study Skills

1. Write three words you could type into your search engine to find more information about twins on the Internet.

   _____

   _____

   _____

Reading Connection—Grade 2—RBP3810   www.summerbridgeactivities.com   ©RBP Books

Opposites

My brother and I are opposites.
Believe me because it's true.

I have brown eyes, but
My brother's eyes are blue.

When I sit, my brother stands.
I sunburn easily, but he tans.

I am quiet. He is loud.
I am humble. He is proud.

I like soft music. He likes rock.
I like to sing. He likes to talk.

Although we're opposites to the end,
My brother still is my best friend.

Reading Skills

1. Even though they are opposites, what does the author say about her brother at the end of the poem?

   A. He is very different.

   B. He is okay.

   C. He is her best friend.

Complete each sentence with either the word <u>brother</u> or <u>sister</u>.

2. The _____ has brown eyes.

3. The _____ has blue eyes.

4. The _____ is quiet.

5. The _____ is loud.

6. The _____ likes to sing.

7. The _____ likes to talk.

Vocabulary Skills

Draw a line between the opposites.

1. brown eyes   tan

2. sit   proud

3. sunburn   loud

4. quiet   blue eyes

5. humble   stand

Language Skills

The words **but** and **and** are conjunctions. They are words that join phrases together. <u>And</u> joins like phrases together. <u>But</u> joins opposite phrases together. Complete each sentence using <u>and</u> or <u>but</u>.

1. I like hot weather, _____ my friend likes the snow.

2. My friend _____ I like to eat hamburgers.

3. I am tall, _____ my friend is short.

4. My friend likes to play soccer, _____ so do I.

Thinking Skills

1. Name two ways you and your friend are opposites.

_____

_____

2. Name two ways you and your friend are the same.

_____

_____

Reading Connection—Grade 2—RBP3810   www.summerbridgeactivities.com   ©RBP Books

Teddy Bear

I'm too old for my teddy bear,
And poor Ted is showing too much wear.

Now that I'm a bigger kid,
It's time that I kept Teddy hid.

So I said "good-bye" to my old friend
Because teddy bears are just pretend.

But that first night, I couldn't sleep,
Though I tried and tried counting sheep.

I thought about my teddy bear,
Hidden in the closet there.

And now I miss old Teddy so,
I just can't let my old friend go.

So I tiptoed quietly out of bed
And found my little bear called Ted,

And I brought him back to bed with me.
Poor Ted still needs me, can't you see?

www.summerbridgeactivities.com   Reading Connection—Grade 2—RBP3810

Reading Skills

1. What is the main idea?
   A. It's hard to give up a teddy bear.
   B. Everybody needs a teddy bear.
   C. Teddy bears are not real.

2. Why does the writer feel it's time to say good-bye to Ted?
   A. He is too old for a teddy bear.
   B. He can't find Ted.
   C. Ted is in the closet.

3. Where was Ted "hiding"?
   A. under the bed
   B. in the closet
   C. in the toy box

Language Skills

1. Find 10 words using only the letters in the word <u>teddy bear</u>.

   _____   _____

   _____   _____

   _____   _____

   _____   _____

   _____   _____

Vocabulary Skills

Draw a line between the rhyming words.

1. bear   pretend

2. kid   see

3. friend   sheep

4. sleep   go

5. so   there

6. bed   hid

7. me   Ted

Write the two words that each **contraction** stands for.

8. I'm   _____   _____

9. it's   _____   _____

10. couldn't   _____   _____

11. I've   _____   _____

Thinking Skills

1. Do you have a favorite toy? How would you feel if you had to give it up?

   _____

   _____

   _____

A Song for My Son

Here's a song for my son. It's a hymn for him. It's about the day my dear son rode away. My son rode on his bike down the road in the sun. He rode and he rode down the road. He rode for a week until his knees felt weak. Then he pressed on his brake to take a break. He ate eight pairs of pears. Then he blew a big blue bubble. That night as the sun set, my son became a knight, and in a faraway land he set sail to see the sea.

Reading Skills

1. How would you describe the poem?

   A. silly

   B. true

   C. serious

2. Who is the poem written about?

   A. the sun

   B. a son

   C. a knight

3. How long did the son ride in this poem?

   A. until he saw the sun

   B. until he got to the sea

   C. for a week

Vocabulary Skills

Write a **homonym** for each word.

1. hymn _____

2. sun _____

3. rode _____

4. week _____

5. brake _____

6. ate _____

7. pair _____

8. blew _____

9. night _____

10. see _____

Language Skills

Circle the correct **homonym** in each sentence.

1. The boys (ate   eight) the whole pie.

2. The (sun   son) rises in the east every morning.

3. My favorite color is (blew   blue).

4. I got a new (pair   pear) of shoes.

5. The (rode   road) was very bumpy.

Study Skills

Number these **homonyms** in alphabetical order.

1. _____ son

   _____ sun

   _____ ate

   _____ eight

2. _____ blue

   _____ blew

   _____ break

   _____ brake

3. _____ pair

   _____ pear

   _____ night

   _____ knight

The Synonym Song

Sometimes I talk, but other times I…
shout, whisper, yell, discuss, chatter, or gab.

Sometimes I walk, but other times I…
saunter, tromp, march, step, stroll, trudge, or trek.

Sometimes I run, but other times I…
skip, dash, flee, race, scramble, or scurry.

Sometimes I jump, but other times I…
leap, hop, spring, bound, or vault.

Sometimes I laugh, but other times I…
giggle, chuckle, titter, cackle, roar, or
snicker.

Sometimes I sleep, but other times I…
slumber, rest, doze, nap, or snooze.

Reading Skills

1. What is a <u>synonym</u>?
   A. a word that means the opposite of another word
   B. a word that sounds like another word but has a different meaning
   C. a word that means the same or about the same as another word

Vocabulary Skills

Draw a line between the **synonyms**.

1. talk   leap
2. walk   snooze
3. run   giggle
4. jump   chatter
5. laugh   stroll
6. sleep   dash

Circle the best word in each sentence.

7. I will (whisper   shout) a secret in your ear.

8. I will (saunter   march) to the rhythm of the drum.

9. I will (skip   dash) to get some help.

10. I will (giggle   cackle) in my witch's costume.

11. I will (slumber   nap) all night.

12. I (chuckled   cackled) at the comic in the newspaper.

Study Skills

A **thesaurus** is a book that includes synonyms of words. You can use a thesaurus to make your writing more interesting. Look at this page from a thesaurus. Answer the questions below.

> **sad** (adj): unhappy, down, dismal, morose, miserable, cheerless, gloomy, forlorn, dejected, glum, depressed
> **said** (v): spoke, repeated, harped, yelled, whispered, echoed, bellowed, whined, shouted, told, sang, hammered, mentioned

1. Are the synonyms for the entry word in alphabetical order? _____

2. What does the **(adj)** after the word <u>sad</u> tell you about the word? _____
   _____

3. Rewrite this sentence using a synonym for the word <u>sad</u>. *The boy was feeling sad because he lost his puppy.* _____
   _____

Thinking Skills

1. Write at least four **synonyms** for the word <u>big</u>.
   _____
   _____
   _____
   _____

We have a nickname for my mother's sister. We call her Aunt Antonym because she always says and does the opposite of what we say or do. At the zoo we began at the north end of the park. My aunt began at the south end. At the monkey cage, we thought the monkeys were adorable. My aunt thought they were disgusting. I said a zebra is a white horse with black stripes. My aunt said a zebra is a black horse with white stripes. At the dolphin show we sat in the front. We like getting wet. My aunt sat in the back. She wanted to stay dry. Soon we were hungry. My aunt was still full from breakfast. After lunch we rode the train around the zoo. My aunt wanted to walk. Finally, my aunt said she was ready to go. We wished we could have stayed.

Reading Skills

Write **T** before the statements that are true and **F** before the statements that are false.

1. _____ The author is writing about his sister.

2. _____ Aunt Antonym is the real name of the author's aunt.

3. _____ Aunt Antonym thinks monkeys are disgusting.

4. _____ Aunt Antonym wanted to sit in the back at the dolphin show because she didn't like to get wet.

Answer in a complete sentence.

5. Why did the author call his aunt Aunt Antonym? _____

_____

Vocabulary Skills

An **antonym** is a word that means the opposite of another word. For example, an antonym of big is little. Write a word from the story that is an antonym for each word below.

1. north _____

2. disgusting _____

3. black _____

4. front _____

5. dry _____

6. hungry _____

Language Skills

Write the **past tense** for each verb.

1. begin _____

2. think _____

3. say _____

4. ride _____

5. sit _____

Study Skills

This bar graph shows which zoo animals the second graders at Monte Vista School like best. Use the graph to answer the questions below.

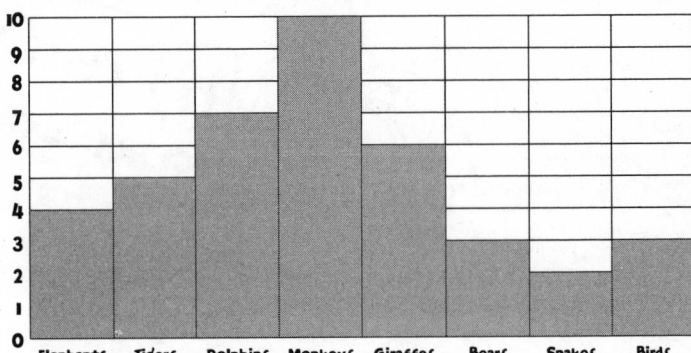

1. Which animal did the most children like? _____

2. Which animal did the fewest children like? _____

3. Besides bears, what animal did three children like? _____

4. Did more children like giraffes or elephants? _____

This year the students at Washington Elementary want every family to join the PTA. Every class has the goal of 100% membership. Read the graph below. Answer the questions that follow.

The PTA Challenge:

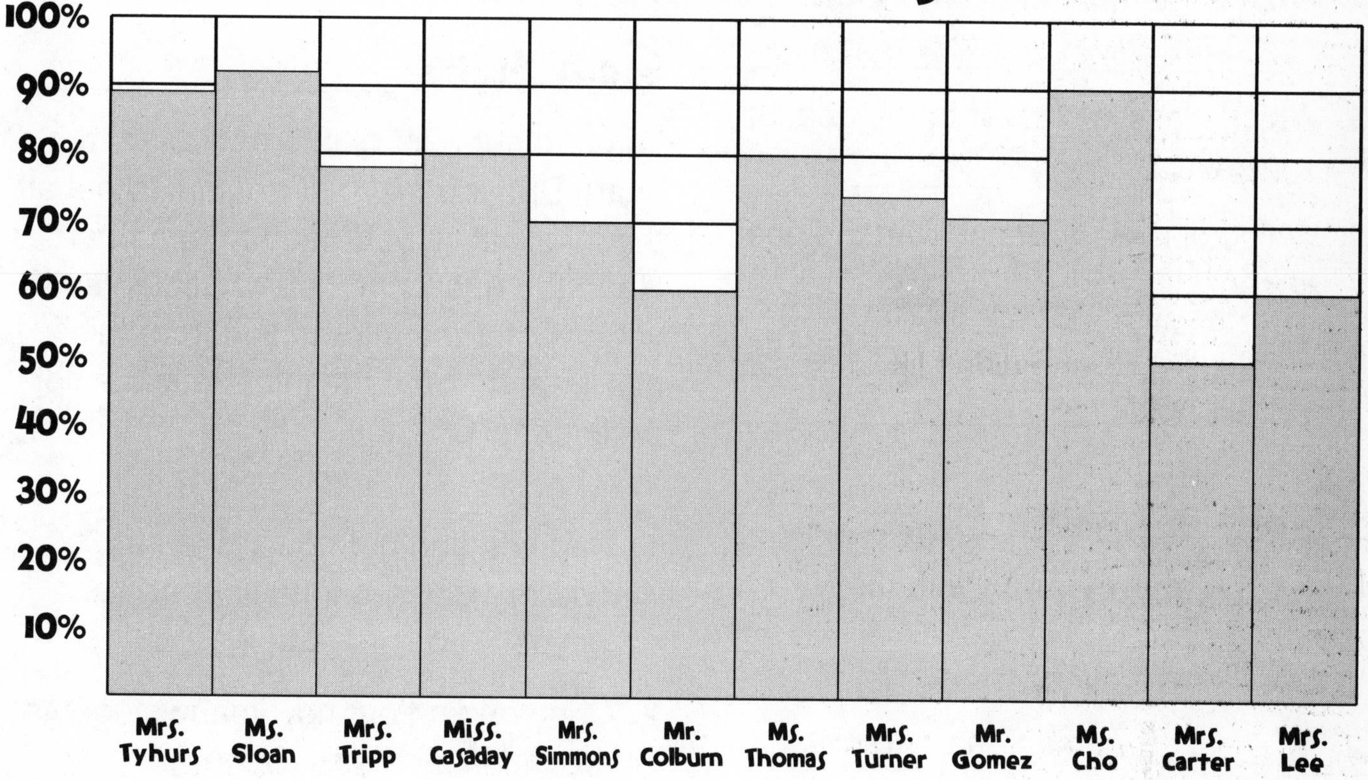

	Mrs. Tyhurs	Ms. Sloan	Mrs. Tripp	Miss. Casaday	Mrs. Simmons	Mr. Colburn	Ms. Thomas	Mrs. Turner	Mr. Gomez	Ms. Cho	Mrs. Carter	Mrs. Lee
100%												
90%												
80%												
70%												
60%												
50%												
40%												
30%												
20%												
10%												

Our Goal Is 100% Membership!

Reading Skills

Use the graph to answer the questions.

1. What is the title of the graph?

   _____

2. What is the goal of each class?

   _____

3. Which class is closest to the goal of 100%? _____

4. Which class is furthest from the goal of 100%? _____

5. Which two classes have reached 80% of their goal? _____

Vocabulary Skills

Match the **abbreviation** with the meaning.

1. Mrs.   unmarried woman

2. Mr.   woman, married or unmarried

3. Dr.   married woman

4. Miss.   man

5. Ms.   doctor, man or woman

Language Skills

Fill in each blank with the **possessive** form of the name in parentheses.

1. (Mrs. Simmons) _____
   class has reached 70% of its goal.

2. (Ms. Sloan) _____
   class has 27 students.

3. (Ms. Turner) _____ class
   is closer to its goal than (Mr. Gomez)
   _____ class.

4. (Miss Casaday) _____
   class had three students absent.

Study Skills

You can get a lot of information from a chart. But you may not be able to get all the information you need from a chart. Read the questions below. Circle **yes** if you can get the information from this chart. Circle **no** if the information is not on the chart.

1. Can you find out how close Mrs. Tyhurs's class is to their goal?
   yes   no

2. Can you find out how many students are in Mr. Gomez's class?
   yes   no

3. Can you tell whether Mrs. Lee's class or Mrs. Tripp's class is closer their goal?
   yes   no

4. Can you figure out how many more families must join the PTA for the school to reach its goal?
   yes   no

5. Can you tell the names of the students in Ms. Cho's class?
   yes   no

Television Schedule

The Lori Show

	7:00	7:30	8:00	8:30	9:00	9:30	10:00	10:30
2	Make a Million Game Show	Jump Start		Cops and Robbers			News	
4	Lucky Guess	You Should Know	Wednesday Night at the Movies "Friends Forever"				News	
5	Best Friends	Mary's Secret	Where They Are	Time to Hope	Tom's Talk Show		News	
7	123 Oak Street	Lost Alone	One More Time		Sports		News	
11	Your Health	Eating Right	Food News		Cooking with Kate		Home Decorating	Shopping Now
24	Silly Rabbit	Clyde the Clown	Balls o' Fun	Slime & Rhyme	Cartoon Alley		Fun Times	Make Me Laugh

www.summerbridgeactivities.com

Reading Skills

Circle the correct answer.

1. What does this schedule show?
   A. times and channels of television shows
   B. times and channels of radio programs
   C. the number of people that like different shows

2. On what channels can you watch news at 10:00?
   A. 2, 5, and 11
   B. 3, 4, and 11
   C. 2, 4, 5, and 7

3. What time is the show *Silly Rabbit*?
   A. 7:00
   B. 7:30
   C. 8:30

4. What is the Wednesday night movie?
   A. *Lost Alone*
   B. *Mary's Secret*
   C. *Friends Forever*

Vocabulary Skills

Circle the word that does not belong.

1. food   cook   decorate   eat
2. slime   rhyme   clown   time
3. talk   whisper   laugh   shout
4. know   guess   predict   suggest
5. funny   serious   humorous   silly

Language Skills

Add the suffix **-ing** to the following words:

1. shop _____
2. decorate _____
3. eat _____
4. laugh _____
5. cook _____

Study Skills

1. Number the shows in alphabetical order.
   ____ *Make a Million*
   ____ *Lucky Guess*
   ____ *Mary's Secret*
   ____ *Make Me Laugh*

Signs

Signs are everywhere. Signs help people. Some signs tell you to stop. Some signs tell you to be careful. Some signs tell you where to enter. Some signs tell you not to enter. Some signs tell you where to leave. Read signs. Follow the directions on the signs. Signs are helpful.

A.

B.

C.

D.

E.

F.

G.

H.

www.summerbridgeactivities.com Reading Connection—Grade 2—RBP3810

Reading Skills

1. What is the main idea?

   A. Signs are helpful.

   B. Signs get in the way.

   C. Signs are hard to read.

2. Place the letter of the sign on
   page 79 next to what the sign means.

   _____ exit

   _____ train tracks

   _____ girls' bathroom

   _____ be careful

   _____ boys' bathroom

   _____ enter here

   _____ stop

   _____ yield the right of way

Vocabulary Skills

Draw lines between the opposites.

1. stop   girl

2. boy   careless

3. enter   go

4. everywhere   exit

5. careful   nowhere

Thinking Skills

1. Draw a sign that would be helpful at
   your school.

The Circus Is Coming
June 15 – June 22
Show times: 3:00 and 7:00

The Greatest Show Around!

Trapeze Artists
Animals
Tightrope Walkers
Fire Eaters
Clowns

Food and Fun for the Whole Family

Tickets cost:
$7.50 for adults
$5.00 for children
Children two and under are FREE!

Reading Skills

1. What is the poster about?

   A. Clowns are funny.

   B. Have fun with your family.

   C. The circus is coming.

2. Draw a line between the person and how much it costs the person to go to the circus.

   adults $5.00

   children   free

   children two and under $7.50

3. Put a √ by the details that are true.

   _____ The circus will be in town on June 20th.

   _____ There will be clowns at the circus.

   _____ There are no tightrope walkers at the circus.

   _____ You can see the circus at either 3:00 or 7:00.

   _____ Children under two should not come to the circus.

Language Skills

Sentences tell a complete thought. A sentence tells you who and what. Put an **S** by the sentences below. Put an **N** if it is not a sentence.

1. The circus is coming to town. _____

2. Food and fun for the whole family. ___

3. Children under two are free. _____

4. The greatest show around. _____

5. I love the circus. _____

Thinking Skills

1. Put the animals in the right group.

   pig   **elephant**   **tiger**

   lion   **cow**   **chicken**

   Circus Animals

   _____

   _____

   _____

   Farm Animals

   _____

   _____

   _____

Always be sure to read the label on a product. Labels provide warnings, first aid instructions, and instructions for how to use a product safely. If used properly, most products are safe. However, if not used properly, many products can be dangerous.

Labels explain ① what the product should be used for, ② what is in the product, ③ warnings about what may happen if the product is not used properly, and ④ who to contact if you have questions about a product.

Some key words to look for when reading a label include: NOTE, WARNING, KEEP OUT OF REACH OF CHILDREN, DANGER, POISON, and CAUTION. Pay special attention to the words that follow these warnings.

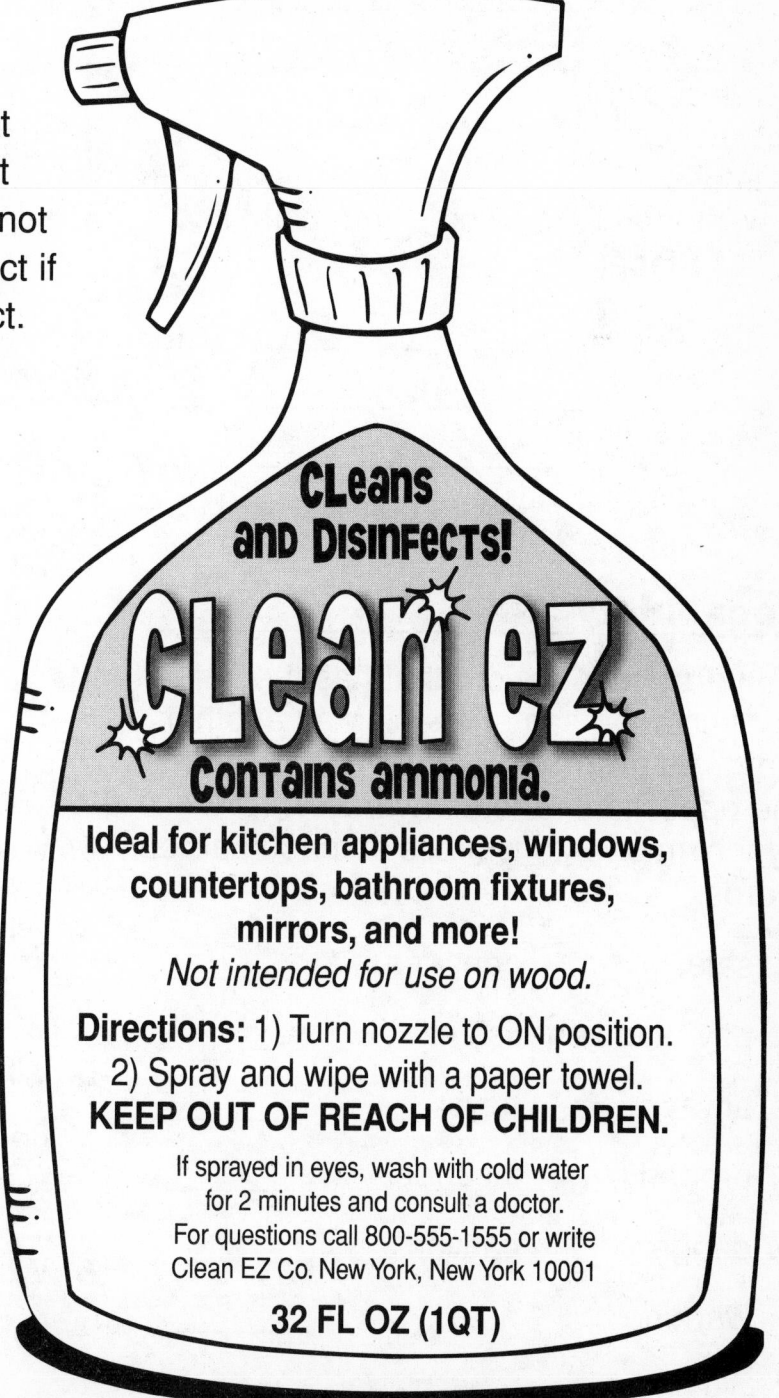

CLeans and DisinfeCts!

cLean ez

Contains ammonia.

Ideal for kitchen appliances, windows, countertops, bathroom fixtures, mirrors, and more!
Not intended for use on wood.

Directions: 1) Turn nozzle to ON position.
2) Spray and wipe with a paper towel.
KEEP OUT OF REACH OF CHILDREN.

If sprayed in eyes, wash with cold water
for 2 minutes and consult a doctor.
For questions call 800-555-1555 or write
Clean EZ Co. New York, New York 10001

32 FL OZ (1QT)

Reading Skills

Read the label. Answer the following questions.

1. Give three reason you should always read a label on a product before you use it.

   _____

   _____

   _____

2. Write three key words you might find on a label.

   _____

   _____

   _____

Vocabulary Skills

A **synonym** is a word that has the same or almost the same meaning as another word. An **antonym** is a word that means the opposite of another word. Write <u>synonym</u> or <u>antonym</u> beside each pair of words.

1. safe   dangerous   _____

2. pay attention listen   _____

3. always   never   _____

4. properly   incorrectly   _____

5. danger   caution   _____

6. warning   note   _____

Language Skills

Place an **exclamation point** (**!**) at the end of the sentences below that show excitement. Place a **period** (**.**)at the end of the rest of the sentences.

1. Danger   Do Not Enter

2. Run and get help

3. Today is Saturday

4. Don't touch the hot stove

5. My brother is 3 years older than me

Study Skills

Read the label and answer the questions.

1. What is the name of the product?

   _____

2. What should the product be used for?

   _____

3. What is in the product? _____

4. What warning does the product give?

   _____

5. What number should you call if you have questions about the product?

   _____

6. Would the product be good to clean your wood coffee table? _____

Here's your mission, should you choose to accept it!

come TO a SPY BIRTHDAY

For: Josh's 9th Birthday
When: Saturday, September 13th
Time: 4:00-6:00
Where: Papa's Pizza Palace

R.S.V.P. by September 10th
to 444-5544.

Reading Skills

Read the invitation. Answer the following questions.

1. Who is the party for? _____

2. What is the party for? _____

3. When is the party? _____

4. Where is the party? _____

5. By what date should you R.S.V.P.?

_____

Vocabulary Skills

Circle the answer that tells the meaning of the following words as used in the invitation. Use a dictionary if you need to.

1. <u>mission</u>

   A. old church building

   B. to do church work in other lands

   C. a job that must be done

2. <u>accept</u>

   A. to answer "yes"

   B. to say anything but what is expected

   C. to wait

3. <u>R.S.V.P.</u>

   A. really silly violin party

   B. reply to the invitation

   C. be sure to buy a present

Language Skills

An **apostrophe** (')is used to show possessives and contractions. Write a **P** if the apostrophe shows the possessive and a **C** if the apostrophe is in a contraction.

1. you're _____

2. Josh's _____

3. here's _____

4. Papa's Pizza Palace _____

Study Skills

Use the table of contents below to answer the questions.

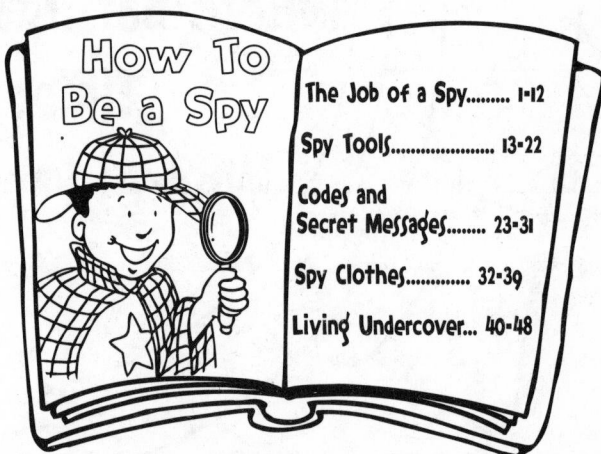

1. What is the title of the second chapter? _____

2. On what pages would you look to find information on what a spy should wear? _____

3. What chapter would you read to find out more about what a spy does?

_____

4. On what page would you start reading about the tools a spy uses? _____

Reading Connection—Grade 2—RBP3810   www.summerbridgeactivities.com   ©**RBP Books**

June 21, 2003

Dear Grandma and Grandpa,

What's happening? I'm just chilling. Today is the first day of my summer vacation. I have some radical things planned this summer. Tomorrow I start swimming lessons. Then later on today, my friend Michael is coming over. We're going to ride our bikes. Mom said that in two weeks we are going to visit you. I can't wait. Can we go to the park with the waterslides? I had a blast last year when we went there. Also, I want to go fishing with Grandpa. This year I'm going to catch the biggest fish. You'll have to buy a new pan to cook it in because I don't think the pans you have are big enough. Well, I have to split. Catch you later.

Love, Nick

Reading Skills

Read the letter. Answer the following questions.

1. Who is the letter to? _____
   _____

2. Who is the letter from? _____
   _____

3. Name two things that Nick is going to do this summer. _____
   _____
   _____

Vocabulary Skills

Language between friends and family often includes slang words and phrases. **Slang** words are informal words that should not be used in formal speech or writing. Draw lines to match each slang word to its meaning.

1. What's happening?   A. go

2. chilling   B. See you soon.

3. blast   C. How are you?

4. split   D. relaxing

5. Catch you later.   E. fun

Language Skills

Write the two words that make up each **contraction**.

1. what's _____ _____

2. I'm   _____ _____

3. we're _____ _____

4. can't _____ _____

5. you'll _____ _____

6. I'll   _____ _____

Thinking Skills

1. Make a list of things you would like to do on your next summer vacation.

   _____
   _____
   _____
   _____
   _____
   _____
   _____

The Mouse and His Food

Fables *are short stories with a* *moral.* *A moral is a lesson. Most fables have animal characters. This story is an example of a fable.*

One day a little mouse sat inside his little house inside a log. "Oh dear," said the mouse. "I have nothing to eat but this small seed. Surely I will starve." So the little mouse set out to find some food.

Soon the little mouse found two acorns. He took the acorns to his house. "Oh dear," said the mouse. "I have nothing to eat but these two acorns and a small seed. What if the rains come and wash them away? Surely I will starve." So the little mouse set out to find more food.

Soon he found a corn cob. He took the cob back to his house. "Oh dear," said the mouse. "I have nothing to eat but these two acorns, a small seed, and this corn cob. What if the winds come and blow them away? Surely I will starve." So the little mouse set out to find more food.

Soon he found six walnuts. He took the walnuts back to his house. "Oh dear," said the mouse. "I have nothing to eat but these two acorns, this small seed, this corn cob, and these six walnuts. What if the snows come and freeze them all? Surely I will starve." So the little mouse set out to find more food.

This went on for days. Finally, the mouse had gathered more food than ten mice could eat in a year. Soon the rains and the wind and the snow did come. But none of the food was washed away. None of the food blew away. And none of the food froze. But because the mouse could not eat all the food, the food rotted. Because the mouse could not eat rotten food, he starved.

© RBP Books   www.summerbridgeactivities.com   Reading Connection—Grade 2—RBP3810

Reading Skills

Circle the correct answer.

1. What is the <u>moral,</u> or lesson, of this story?

   A. Weather can ruin your plans.

   B. Storing up more than you need may cause you problems.

   C. A mouse doesn't eat very much food.

2. What word best describes the mouse?

   A. friendly

   B. hungry

   C. fearful

3. What is the mouse afraid of?

   A. starving

   B. being eaten by a cat

   C. being washed away by the rain

4. What happened to the mouse's food?

   A. It blew away.

   B. It rotted.

   C. The mouse ate it.

5. What happened to the mouse?

   A. He starved.

   B. He had enough food to eat.

   C. He shared the food that he gathered.

Vocabulary Skills

Homonyms (or **homophones**) are words that sound the same but have different meanings and spellings. Find a homonym in the fable for each word below.

1. won _____

2. deer _____

3. sum _____

4. too _____

5. daze _____

6. blue _____

7. sew _____

8. reins _____

Language Skills

Write the plural of each word below.

1. mouse _____

2. acorn _____

3. house _____

4. year _____

5. day _____

Study Skills

1. Aesop wrote many fables. If you wanted to find out more about Aesop, what two words could you type into a search engine on the Internet?

   _____

   _____

The Ants and the Cookies

One day two ants went exploring. They came across two giant cookies.

"These cookies are huge!" said the first ant.

"One of these cookies would feed my whole family for a month," said the second ant. "But how can such little ants like us carry such big cookies like these?"

"It seems impossible!" said the first little ant. "But I must try."

So the first little ant started to tug and pull at the cookie. Suddenly a tiny piece broke from the cookie.

"I am going to take this piece back to my family," said the first little ant.

"You go ahead," said the second little ant. "I'm not going to waste my time on such a small piece of cookie. I will find a way to take the whole cookie back to my family."

So away the first ant went with his small piece of cookie. Soon the first ant returned. He found the second ant still pushing and shoving at the cookie. He was unable to budge it. Again the first little ant broke off a small piece of cookie and took it back to his family. This went on for most of the day. The first little ant kept carrying small bits of cookie back to his family until the entire cookie had been moved. The second little ant finally tired of trying to complete a task that seemed too big to do. He went home with nothing.

Reading Skills

Circle the correct answer.

1. You can tell this story is a fable because

    A. it is short.

    B. it has a moral.

    C. it has animals as characters.

    D. all of the above.

2. What is the moral of the story?

    A. Sometimes the best way to handle a big job is a little bit at a time.

    B. Some tasks are just too big for ants.

    C. Ants like cookies.

3. How did the first little ant carry the cookie home?

    A. He dragged it.

    B. He carried a little bit at a time.

    C. He ate most of it first.

4. What happened to the second little ant?

    A. He got tired of trying and quit.

    B. He carried the cookie home.

    C. He ate the cookie.

Vocabulary Skills

Synonyms are words that have almost the same meaning. Draw lines between the synonyms.

1. giant	whole
2. tug	move
3. tiny	huge
4. budge	shove
5. entire	little
6. push	pull

Language Skills

Write the **past tense** for each action word.

1. come _____

2. feed _____

3. start _____

4. go _____

5. say _____

6. take _____

7. move _____

8. break _____

Three Wishes

A long time ago, there lived a little old woman and a little old man. They didn't have much money. But they did have a fine little house and enough food on the table. One day the couple went fishing. They sat for hours without one bite. Suddenly, the man felt a tug on his line. He reeled in the fish. What a big fish it was. Surely, this fish would feed him and his wife for a whole week. But as began to unhook the fish, the fish spoke!

"Please let me go," said the fish. "If you do, I will grant you three wishes."

"A talking fish!" shouted the old man. "How can this be?" And without thinking, he threw the fish back into the water.

The little old woman shouted, "You foolish man. You threw the fish back without making any wishes. And you threw back a fish that could feed us for a week. Just once I wish you would think!"

Just as the words came out of the woman's mouth, a thought popped in the man's mind. "Well," said the man, "your wish has come true. I am thinking. I am thinking you are a rude woman, and I wish you would keep quiet!"

And just as the man wished, the woman's mouth was shut tight. The old couple sat there staring at each other. "What have we done?" the man said. "With three wishes we could have wished for money, food, or fame, but instead we wished away our wishes. Now the only sensible wish would be that my wife's mouth would be opened."

And as quickly as the man said the last wish, the woman's mouth was opened. "We don't have money or food or fame, but we do have each other. And that is enough," said the old man. Together the little old woman and the little old man walked silently back to their house.

93

Reading Skills

Circle the correct answer.

1. What is the main idea?

    A. Be careful not to catch talking fish.

    B. Think before you speak.

    C. Always be ready with three wishes.

2. How would you describe this story?

    A. serious

    B. true

    C. silly

Read the sentences. Write **T** if it might be true. Write **F** if it is fantasy or make-believe.

3. _____ A long time ago, there lived an old man and an old woman.

4. _____ The couple went fishing.

5. _____ The man caught a talking fish.

6. _____ The woman's mouth shut tight.

7. _____ The couple walked back to their house.

Vocabulary Skills

A **homonym** (or **homophone**) is a word that sounds the same as another word but has a different spelling and meaning. Write a homonym from the story for each word below.

1. ours _____

2. real _____

3. weak _____

4. bee _____

5. through _____

Language Skills

Use correct punctuation at the end of each sentence.

1. Have you ever seen a talking fish ____

2. That fish can talk _____

3. My dad caught a fish _____

4. Can you go fishing with me _____

5. I like to go fishing with my dad _____

Thinking Skills

1. If you had three wishes, what would they be?

_____

_____

_____

Gingerbread Boy

One day a woman decided to bake some gingerbread. Since the woman had no children of her own, she decided to make her gingerbread into the shape of a boy. She placed raisins where the eyes should be and licorice for the mouth. She used little cinnamon drops for the buttons on his vest. When she was satisfied, she popped her little gingerbread boy into the oven. Soon she could smell the delicious scent of warm gingerbread. She opened the oven door, and out popped a little gingerbread boy.

"Mmmm. You smell delicious," sighed the old woman. "Run, run, as fast as you can. You can't catch me. I'm too fast, you see!" the gingerbread boy laughed and off he ran. "Oh my," screamed the little old woman, and off she ran after her little gingerbread boy.

The little gingerbread boy came to a young boy. "Mmmm. You smell delicious," shouted the boy. But the gingerbread boy just laughed and said, " Run, run, as fast as you can. You can't catch me. I'm too fast, you see!" And off ran the little gingerbread boy with the little old woman and the boy close behind.

The little gingerbread boy came to a girl. "Mmmm. You smell delicious," squealed the girl. But the gingerbread boy just laughed and said, "Run, run, as fast as you can. You can't catch me. I'm too fast, you see!" And off ran the gingerbread boy with the old woman, the boy, and the girl close behind.

Soon the gingerbread boy came to a man. "Mmmm. You smell delicious," bellowed the man. But the gingerbread boy just laughed and said, "Run, run, as fast as you can. You can't catch me. I'm too fast, you see!" And off ran the gingerbread boy with the old woman, the boy, the girl, and the man close behind.

Soon the gingerbread boy came to a river. "Oh dear," said the gingerbread boy. "How will I cross this river?"

"I'll give you a ride," snickered the alligator with a sly smile. "Just jump on my back."

Seeing as the gingerbread boy was new to the ways of the world he accepted the offer of the alligator. And as you might expect, the gingerbread boy didn't make it across the river, but instead into the belly of the alligator.

When the old woman, the boy, the girl, and the man reached the river, they knew immediately what had happened. "Let's go home," sighed the old woman. "I will make us some gingerbread. Just a plain loaf of gingerbread."

© RBP Books — www.summerbridgeactivities.com — Reading Connection—Grade 2—RBP3810

Reading Skills

1. Number the sentences in the order they happened in the story.

_____ The old woman baked a plain loaf of gingerbread.

_____ The old woman chased the gingerbread boy.

_____ The old woman cut her ginger-bread into the shape of a boy.

_____ The boy chased the ginger-bread boy.

_____ The alligator ate the ginger-bread boy.

_____ The girl chased the gingerbread boy.

_____ The man chased the ginger-bread boy.

_____ The gingerbread boy came to a river.

Vocabulary Skills

1. Look back in the story. Find 6 words that were used in place of the word <u>said</u> in the story.

_____

_____

_____

_____

_____

Study Skills

Read the recipe. Answer the questions.

Gingerbread Cookies

1 cup molasses   1/2 cup brown sugar
1/3 cup water   1/3 cup shortening
6 cups flour   1 tsp. baking soda
2 tsp. ginger   1 tsp. cinnamon
1 tsp. allspice

1. Mix together molasses, brown sugar, water, and shortening.

2. Sift together flour, soda, and spices. Then add to molasses mixture. Cover and refrigerate overnight.

3. Heat oven to 350°. Roll out dough on a floured board. Use cookie cutters to cut shapes. Place cookies on a cookie sheet. Bake 10–12 minutes.

Makes 2 dozen cookies.

1. What type of cookies does this recipe make? _____

2. How many cups of flour will you need? _____

3. Name the three spices used in this recipe. _____

_____

_____

4. How hot should the oven be? _____

5. How long do you need to refrigerate the dough? _____

6. How long do you need to bake the cookies? _____

7. How many cookies will this recipe make? _____

Pickled Potato Pancakes

Once upon a time, in a kingdom far away, lived a prince named Peter. Prince Peter had a pony named Pepper. Pepper would eat only pickled potato pancakes. One day the royal kitchen ran out of pickled potato pancakes.

"What? No pickled potato pancakes," shouted the prince. "What will we do?"

"I will search throughout the land," declared the prince's faithful servant, Patrick. "I will not return until I have found some pickled potato pancakes."

Needless to say, it was not easy to find such a food. Patrick searched far and wide. He explored kingdom after kingdom. He hunted in caves and coves. But no pickled potato pancakes were to be found. Then one day Patrick came upon a castle deep within the forest. The castle was painted a pleasant shade of pink. In this castle lived a beautiful princess. Her name was Penelope. Penelope lived alone with her pet pig named Porky. Patrick was hungry from his long journey. So Patrick approached the pink castle that belonged to Princess Penelope.

"May I have a bite to eat?" questioned Patrick.

The princess giggled. "I'm sorry," said the princess, "but the only thing I know how to make is pickled potato pancakes. It's all my Porky will eat."

Now it was Patrick's turn to laugh. "You are just what I am looking for," chuckled Patrick. Patrick told the princess his story and asked her if she would come back to the castle with him.

"We are kind of lonely. Sure we'll come," agreed Princess Penelope.

When Princess Penelope, Patrick, and Porky arrived back at the castle, it was love at first sight between the prince and princess. They lived happily ever after, making pickled potato pancakes for Peter's pony, Penelope, and the princess's pig, Porky.

© RBP Books   www.summerbridgeactivities.com   Reading Connection—Grade 2—RBP3810

Reading Skills

1. All fairy tales are fantasy, or make-believe. Put a √ by the statements that make this story a fairy tale.

_____ Once upon a time, in a kingdom far away …

_____ Prince Peter had a pony named Pepper.

_____ Pepper ate only pickled potato pancakes.

_____ He hunted in caves and coves.

_____ The castle was painted a pleasant shade of pink.

_____ They lived happily ever after.

Vocabulary Skills

Draw lines between the **synonyms**. Remember, synonyms are words that mean about the same thing.

1. explored   laughed
2. giggled   hunted
3. declared   questioned
4. beautiful   pretty
5. asked   shouted

Language Skills

Alliteration means using the same beginning sounds. The p-sounds in *Prince Peter's pony Pepper* are an example of alliteration. On each line below, write two words that start like the word at the beginning of the line.

1. bear _____

2. silly_____

3. turtle _____

4. dog_____

Study Skills

Although this story is a fantasy, princes and castles are real. Use the encyclopedias below. Write the number of the volume where you would find the following information.

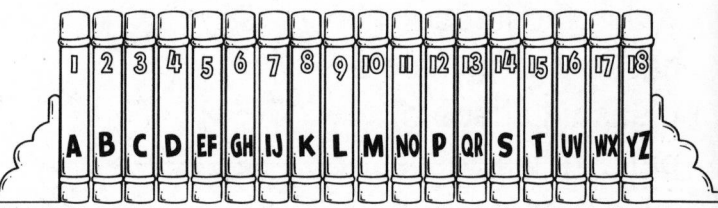

1. Prince Phillip _____

2. castles _____

3. Queen Elizabeth _____

4. knights _____

The Frugal King

In a kingdom faraway lived a frugal king. Each week the king put some of his kingdom's food into a large storehouse in the castle. The people of the kingdom complained.

"Why does the king take our food and store it away?" questioned one of the townspeople.

"I bet he is taking our food and eating it himself," accused another.

"We are starving," exaggerated another. "We barely have enough to eat."

"All the people from the kingdom on the other side of the land eat until their stomachs almost burst," shouted another. "Our king is cruel to his people."

Despite the complaining, the king continued to take a portion of the food and store it away.

The complaining continued until one day there came a famine in the land. The famine made it impossible to grow wheat to make bread. The famine made it impossible to feed the cows, so there was no milk or cheese. The townspeople in kingdoms throughout the land were starving to death. But the people from the frugal king's kingdom had plenty to eat. The king opened the doors of the storehouses and fed his people. The townspeople knew that the king's frugalness saved their lives.

www.summerbridgeactivities.com

Reading Connection—Grade 2—RBP3810

Reading Skills

1. How did the townspeople feel about the king at the beginning of the story?

   A. They were proud of the king.

   B. They thought the king was mean and selfish.

   C. They thought the king was fat.

2. How did the people feel about the king at the end of the story?

   A. They thought the king was mean and selfish.

   B. They thought the king was rich.

   C. They were grateful to the king.

3. What problem did the famine not cause?

   A. There was no milk or cheese.

   B. There was no water to drink.

   C. There was no wheat to make bread.

Language Skills

Use the verb **is** with a singular subject. Use the verb **are** with a plural subject. Write is or are to complete the sentences below.

1. The king_____frugal.

2. We _____starving.

3. They _____working hard.

4. The townspeople_____complaining.

5. The boy _____hungry.

Vocabulary Skills

1. From this story, the word <u>frugal</u> means _____.

   A. mean

   B. careful

   C. selfish

2. From this story, the word <u>famine</u> means _____.

   A. a wild beast

   B. food shortage

   C. special holiday

3. Circle the words that mean the same as <u>cruel</u>.

   unkind   loving

   mean   uncaring

   helpful   heartless

   nice   harsh

Thinking Skills

1. Write your own fairy tale. Remember to include royalty and lots of fantasy.

The Swing

How do you like to go up in a swing,
Up in the air so blue?
Oh, I do think it the pleasantest thing
Ever a child can do!

Up in the air and over the wall,
Till I can see so wide,
Rivers and trees and cattle and all
Over the countryside—

Till I look down on the garden green,
Down on the roof so brown—
Up in the air I go flying again,
Up in the air and down!

Robert Louis Stevenson

© RBP Books   www.summerbridgeactivities.com   Reading Connection—Grade 2—RBP3810

Reading Skills

1. Name three things the child sees when he goes up in the swing.

_____

_____

_____

2. Match the color words to the things they describe in the poem.

A. blue   roof

B. green   air

C. brown   garden

3. This poem has the rhythm of a swing going back and forth. Read the poem aloud to someone else. Try to read it with the rhythm of the swing.

Language Skills

Prepositions are words like <u>up</u> and <u>down</u> that tell position. Circle the prepositions in each sentence.

1. The balloon sailed up.

2. The ball landed on the roof.

3. The boy jumped over the wall.

4. The little boy fell down.

5. The dog is in the house.

Draw lines between the rhyming pairs of words.

6. down   do

7. blue   swing

8. all   brown

9. thing   wall

Vocabulary Skills

The suffix **-est** means most. Add **-est** to the words below.

1. big _____

2. long _____

3. pretty _____

4. nice _____

5. little _____

Study Skills

1. Robert Louis Stevenson has written many wonderful poems. What word would you look up in an encyclopedia to find out more about this man's life?

_____

The Wind

by Robert Louis Stevenson

I saw you toss the kites on high

And blow the birds about the sky;

And all around I heard you pass,

Like ladies' skirts across the grass—

      O wind, a-blowing all day long,

      O wind, that sings so loud a song!

I saw the different things you did,

But always you yourself you hid.

I felt you push, I heard you call,

I could not see yourself at all—

      O wind, a-blowing all day long,

      O wind, that sings so loud a song!

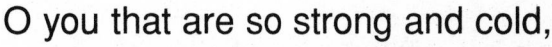

O you that are so strong and cold,

O blower, are you young or old?

Are you a beast of field and tree,

Or just a stronger child than me?

      O wind, a-blowing all day long,

      O wind, that sings so loud a song!

Reading Skills

1. What is this poem about?

   A. flying kites

   B. the wind

   C. playing hide and seek

2. Who is the **you** referring to in the sentence, "I saw **you** toss the kites on high."

   A. the next-door neighbor

   B. the writer of the poem

   C. the wind

3. What did the wind in this poem **not** do?

   A. toss the kites

   B. blow the birds about the sky

   C. tip over the lawn furniture

   D. sing a loud song

Vocabulary Skills

1. In this poem, the word <u>toss</u> means _____.

   A. to mix up like a salad

   B. to throw

   C. to push

2. In this poem, the word <u>beast</u> means _____.

   A. an animal

   B. a monster

   C. an ogre

Language Skills

Write the rhyming word from the poem for each word below.

1. high _____

2. pass _____

3. did _____

4. call _____

5. cold _____

6. tree _____

Thinking Skills

In this poem, the sound of the wind is compared to ladies' skirts across the grass. Think of the sounds below. What could you compare each sound to?

1. a bird singing is like _____

   _____

2. an alarm clock is like _____

   _____

3. a train whistle is like _____

   _____

Playing in the Park

My brother and I like to play in the park by my grandmother's house. Grandmother takes us for walks to the park. My brother goes down the small slide. I go down the big slide. He climbs on the small bars. I climb up the big tower. I twirl on the tire swing. He wants to be pushed on the regular swings. I go across the monkey bars. He feels brave walking across the balance beam. We both try to reach the top of the climbing wall. I go up the difficult course and reach the top. My brother makes it about halfway on the easy course. My brother and I do different things at the park. Even the things we do the same we do differently. But we both have fun.

© RBP Books   www.summerbridgeactivities.com   Reading Connection—Grade 2—RBP3810

Reading Skills

1. You can probably tell that
   A. both children are the same age.
   B. the children make a lot of friends at the park.
   C. the writer of the story is older than her brother.

2. Who takes the children to the park?
   A. the big sister
   B. the grandmother
   C. the mother

3. Who goes down the small slide?
   A. little brother
   B. little sister
   C. grandmother

Vocabulary Skills

Write the two words that make up each **compound word** below.

1. grandmother _____ _____

2. halfway _____ _____

3. ballpark _____ _____

4. waterslide _____ _____

5. playground _____ _____

Language Skills

A **noun** names a person, place, or thing. A **verb** names an action. Some words can be both nouns and verbs. Write **N** under the underlined word if it is a noun. Write **V** if the underlined word is a verb.

1. I play the part of a pirate in the play.
   _____   _____

2. I slide down the big slide.
   _____   _____

3. He swings on the baby swing.
   _____   _____

4. I walk across the bridge on my walk.
   _____   _____

5. My mother mothers my brother and me.
   _____ _____

Thinking Skills

1. Tell about what you like to do at the park. Use complete sentences.

   _____

   _____

   _____

Kate and Her Dad

Kate loves doing things with her dad. He is her best friend. Her dad loves to play basketball. He is on a team. Kate loves to play basketball. She is on a team, too. Her dad is the coach of her team. Sometimes after a game, Kate and her dad go out for ice cream. They both have chocolate fudge rocky road ice cream.

Sometimes before dinner, Kate and her dad go for a run. They run around the track at the neighborhood school.

Kate enjoys running with her dad. Sometimes they talk when they run. Sometimes they just run.

At bedtime, Kate's dad always tucks her in. Kate's dad tells her stories. Her favorite stories are about when her dad was a little boy. Then her dad talks with her about what happened during the day. Then he kisses her gently on the forehead. Kate thinks her dad is the greatest.

www.summerbridgeactivities.com **Reading Connection—Grade 2—RBP3810**

Reading Skills

1. What is this story mainly about?

   A. having fun

   B. why Kate loves her dad

   C. eating ice cream

2. Write three things Kate enjoys doing with her dad.

   _____

   _____

   _____

3. Read the sentences below. Write **S** if the statement is stated in the story. Write **I** if the statement is inferred in the story. **Inferred** means something isn't told exactly, but you get the idea from what is said. Write **U** if the statement is unknown from the story.

   _____ Kate's dad plays on a basketball team.

   _____ Kate's mom plays on a basketball team, too.

   _____ Kate's dad loves her.

   _____ Kate has a little brother.

   _____ Kate's dad always tucks her in.

   _____ Kate and her dad like to talk.

Vocabulary Skills

Write the **plural** of each word.

1. story _____

2. kiss _____

3. hug _____

4. friend _____

5. cone _____

6. neighbor _____

7. boy _____

8. girl _____

Language Skills

Write the two words that make up each **compound word**.

1. basketball   _____ _____

2. bedtime   _____ _____

3. forehead   _____ _____

4. sometimes   _____ _____

Thinking Skills

1. Name three things you like to do with your dad or mom.

   _____

   _____

   _____

What's Big?

Hannah Hippo wanted to be big. But Hannah was the smallest hippo in the jungle. One day Hannah looked at her reflection in the pond. "Look at my teeth. My teeth are big! So I must be big."

Soon a bird came to the pond. "I am big, and I have big teeth," said Hannah. "Yes, you are big," said the bird as it flew away.

Next, a turtle came to the pond. "I am big, and I have big teeth," said Hannah. "Yes, you are big," said the turtle as he sauntered away.

Before long, a baby tiger came to the pond. "I am big, and I have big teeth," said Hannah. "Yes, you are big," said the baby tiger as he scampered away.

Hannah sat by the pond for a long time. "I am big, and I have big teeth. But this is no fun. I have no one to play with." Soon Hannah's mom and dad came to the pond. Hannah looked at her mom and dad. Hannah looked at their big teeth. Hannah felt small. But Hannah didn't mind. At least she had someone to play with. Maybe being small wasn't so bad after all.

www.summerbridgeactivities.com

Reading Skills

1. What did Hannah Hippo want?

   A. for her mom and dad to leave her alone

   B. to be big

   C. to play with the baby tiger

2. Number the sentences as they happened in the story.

   _____ Soon a bird came to the pond.

   _____ Hannah Hippo wanted to be big.

   _____ Hannah's mom and dad came to the pond.

   _____ Next, a turtle came to the pond.

   _____ Before long, a baby tiger came to the pond.

3. Put a **B** by the animals that are bigger than Hannah. Put an **S** by the animals that are smaller than Hannah.

   _____ the turtle

   _____ Hannah's mom

   _____ Hannah's dad

   _____ the bird

   _____ the baby tiger

   _____ all the hippos in the jungle

Vocabulary Skills

Add **-er** or **-est** to the underlined words to complete each sentence.

1. Hannah was <u>small</u> _____ than her dad.

2. Hannah was the <u>small</u> _____ hippo in the jungle.

3. A bird is <u>small</u> _____ than a turtle.

4. Between a tiger, a bird, and a turtle, a bird is the <u>small</u> _____.

Study Skills

Use the encyclopedias below. Write the number of the volume where you would find information on each of the following animals.

1. hippopotamus _____

2. birds _____

3. turtle _____

4. tiger _____

5. jungle animals _____

The Gigantic Cookie

My mother baked a gigantic cookie for me. I sat on my porch to eat it. But before I took a bite, my friend Anna came by.

"Will you share your cookie with me?" Anna asked. So I broke my cookie in two pieces, one for me and one for Anna. But before we took a bite, Jesse and Lucy came by.

"Will you share your cookie with us?" they asked. So Anna and I each broke our cookie pieces in two pieces. Now we had four pieces, one for me, one for Anna, one for Jesse, and one for Lucy. But before we took a bite, four more friends came by.

"Will you share your cookie with us?" they asked. So Anna, Jesse, Lucy, and I all broke our pieces in half. Now we had enough to share with eight friends. But before we took a bite, eight more friends came by.

"Will you share your cookie with us?" they asked. We all broke our pieces in half to share with our eight new friends. I looked at my gigantic cookie. It was no longer gigantic.

"Hey, anyone know what is gigantic when there's one, but small when there are sixteen?" I said.

"No, what?" my friends asked.

"My cookie," I laughed.

Reading Skills

1. What happened to the cookie?

   A. It was shared between friends.

   B. It broke in half.

   C. It ran away.

2. Number the sentences in the order they happened in the story.

   _____ Jesse and Lucy came by.

   _____ Mother baked a cookie.

   _____ Anna came by.

   _____ Four friends came by.

   _____ Eight friends came by.

Vocabulary Skills

1. Circle the words that mean the same as <u>gigantic</u>.

   big   huge

   enormous   delicious

   large   tiny

2. Use a thesaurus to find at least one more word that means the **same** as <u>gigantic</u>.

   _____

3. Write three words that mean the **opposite** of <u>gigantic</u>.

   _____

   _____

   _____

Language Skills

Use the correct end punctuation for each sentence below.

1. My mother baked a cookie for me

2. Will you share your cookie with me

3. Do you like chocolate chip cookies

4. My favorite cookie is a Snickerdoodle

5. How can we divide the cookie between three people

Thinking Skills

1. Draw the cookie; then divide it into sixteen pieces. Try to make the pieces equal sizes.

The Right Pet

"Please, Mom. Please may I have a pet of my own?" asked Jackie. "Well, you have shown that you can be responsible. I guess it's time you had your own pet," said Mother. "Hurray! Let's go!" shouted Jackie.

"But first you need to think about the right pet," said Mother. "The right pet? I don't under-stand," said Jackie.

"The right pet is the right size. The right pet is the right one for you. You need to think about where you will keep your pet. You need to think about how much time you have to care for it," explained Mother.

"Well," said Jackie. "We live in an apartment, so I guess it will need to be small. I want a pet that I can hold. I want a pet that I can cuddle with."

"Now you're thinking," said Mother. "Let's go see what we can find."

Jackie and her mom went to the pet store. Jackie said to the pet store owner, "I am looking for a small pet with fur that I can hold." The pet store owner showed Jackie a puppy. The puppy was small and furry. But Jackie knew it wouldn't always be small and furry. It would grow up to be a big dog.

Jackie looked at a goldfish. "No good," she said. "I can't hold it."

Finally, Jackie saw a gerbil. "This is perfect. It is small. I can hold it. It has fur. I can cuddle with it. This is the right pet for me," said Jackie. Jackie took the pet home. Now the only problem was deciding on just the right name for just the right pet.

Reading Skills

1. What did Jackie want?
   A. a puppy
   B. a pet of her own
   C. something furry

2. What did Jackie's mom want her to think about?
   A. the right pet
   B. how much a pet costs
   C. her school work

3. Which pet did Jackie not look at?
   A. a puppy
   B. a kitten
   C. a goldfish
   D. a gerbil

4. Jackie solved her problem of choosing the right pet. What problem did Jackie still have?
   A. what to feed a gerbil
   B. what to name her pet
   C. where she would put the cage

5. Put a √ by the things you should think about when choosing a pet.
   _____ the size of the pet

   _____ if the pet is thirsty

   _____ where you will keep the pet

   _____ how much care the pet needs

   _____ if the pet needs a bath

Language Skills

Write the two words that make up each **contraction**.

1. it's   _____ _____

2. let's   _____ _____

3. it'll   _____ _____

4. I'm   _____ _____

5. don't   _____ _____

Thinking Skills

1. Describe the pet that is just right for you.

   _____

   _____

   _____

   _____

   _____

   _____

   _____

   _____

The Pumpkin Farm

Every October, Mrs. Lee's class takes a field trip to the pumpkin farm. They walk around the barnyard and through the barn. They see some animals. Then they go for a hayride. A big tractor pulls a large cart of hay. On the hayride they ride through the apple orchard where the workers are picking apples. Later they will make apple-sauce. After the hayride, they go to the pumpkin patch. There are hundreds of pumpkins. Each student picks out a pumpkin to take home. It is always one of the most fun days of the year.

www.summerbridgeactivities.com

Reading Skills

1. What is the main idea?

   A. There are many things to see at a pumpkin farm.

   B. Pumpkins are for Halloween.

   C. Mrs. Lee is a good teacher.

2. Number each sentence in the order it happened in the story.

   _____ They go on a hayride.

   _____ They walk through the barn.

   _____ They see animals.

   _____ Each student picks out a pumpkin to take home.

Language Skills

Circle the **verb**, or the action word, in each sentence.

1. The children walk through the barn.

2. A big tractor pulls the cart.

3. Each student picks a pumpkin.

4. They ride on horses.

5. The children see lots of animals.

6. Mrs. Lee tells the children about the baby chickens.

7. We laugh at the baby pigs.

8. The pumpkins grow really big.

Vocabulary Skills

Use the underlined words to make a **compound word**.

1. A ride in hay is called a

   _____.

2. A yard by the barn is called a

   _____.

3. A sauce made of apples is called

   _____.

4. A house for a dog is called a

   _____.

5. A house for a hen is called a

   _____.

6. A room with a bed is called a

   _____.

Thinking Skills

1. Circle the animals the children may have seen at the farm.

   sheep   horse

   giraffe   hippopotamus

   chickens   cows

2. Name two more animals you could find at a farm.

   _____

Reading Connection—Grade 2—RBP3810   www.summerbridgeactivities.com   ©RBP Books

A Trip to the Zoo

Martha loves going to the zoo. She likes to watch the flamingos stand on one foot. She likes to watch the giraffes nibble leaves from the trees. Martha thinks the gorillas are the most fun to watch. The babies like to make faces at Martha. Two of the baby gorillas like to roll down the hill. Martha wishes that she could roll down the hill with them.

When she grows up, Martha wants to work at the zoo. She wants to help take care of the animals. Until then, she will look forward to her next trip to the zoo!

Reading Skills

1. What is the main idea?

   A. Martha loves going to the zoo.

   B. Martha loves watching gorillas.

   C. Martha loves to take a vacation.

2. Which animals does Martha like to watch the most?

   A. flamingos

   B. giraffes

   C. gorillas

3. Draw a line from the animal to something it does.

   baby gorillas   nibble leaves

   giraffes   roll down the hill

   flamingos   stand on one foot

4. Why does Martha want to work at the zoo when she grows up?

   A. to get in the zoo for free

   B. to earn some money

   C. to care for the animals

5. What animal did Martha probably not see at the zoo?

   A. elephant

   B. tiger

   C. worm

   D. alligator

Vocabulary Skills

1. In the story, the word <u>loves</u> means

   A. has feelings for.

   B. enjoys.

   C. wants.

2. In the story, the word <u>watch</u> means

   A. to observe.

   B. a timepiece.

   C. to guard.

3. In the story, <u>look forward</u> means

   A. to stare straight ahead.

   B. to anticipate.

   C. to not turn around.

Thinking Skills

1. What is your favorite zoo animal? Tell why.

   _____

   _____

   _____

   _____

   _____

   _____

   _____

The Fire Station

Today our class took a field trip to the fire station. First we met Captain Jim. He showed us the big fire trucks. The fire trucks, or <u>fire engines</u>, have many switches and valves. They have many compartments that hold the equipment and tools used to fight fires and help in emergencies.

We saw the large hoses the firefighters use to put out, or <u>extinguish</u> fires. We saw the tall ladders the fire fighters climb to reach high places. We saw the uniforms the firefighters wear when they fight fires. We got to put on their coats, pants, boots, and hats. The clothes fire fighters wear are big and heavy. Frankie fell over because of the weight of the clothes.

Then we got to see where the firefighters live when they are on duty. Inside the fire station there are beds, showers, and a kitchen. The firefighters take turns cooking meals and shopping for food.

Suddenly, we heard a loud siren. The siren meant that there was an emergency. The firefighters quickly jumped on their fire trucks and drove away. It was interesting to see the fire station and learn about the job of a fire-fighter.

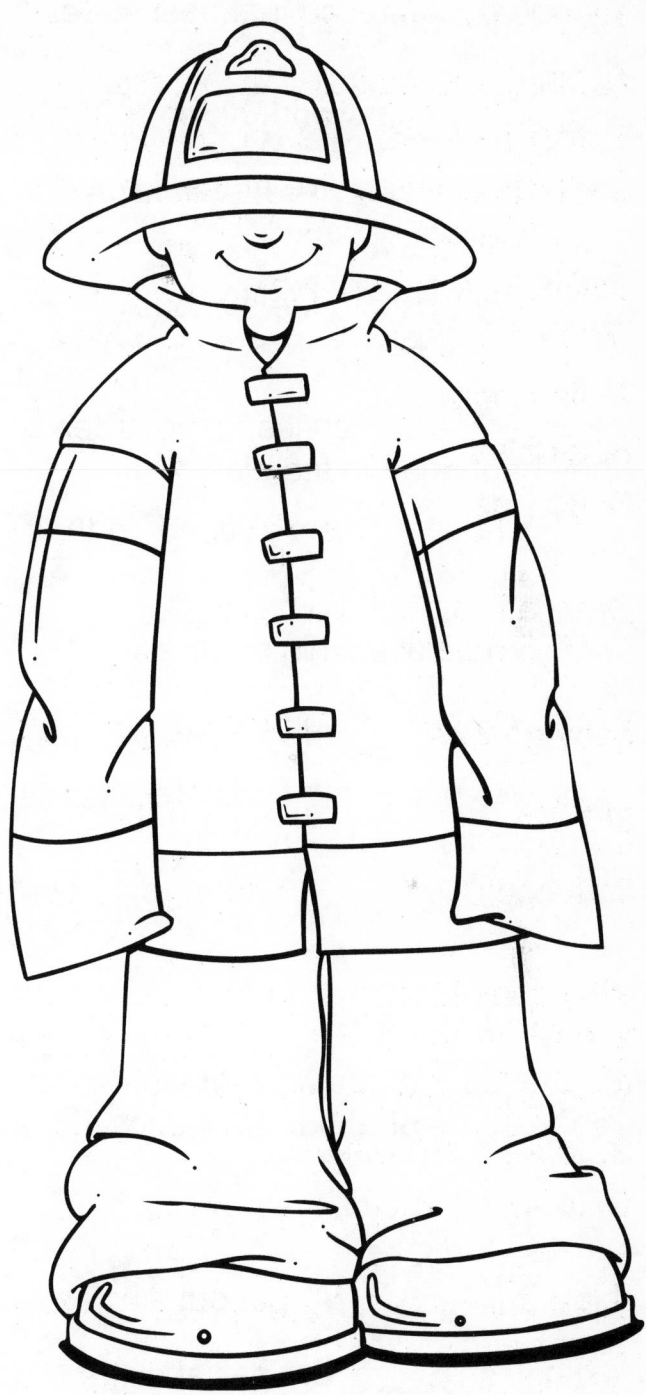

© RBP Books   www.summerbridgeactivities.com   Reading Connection—Grade 2—RBP3810

Reading Skills

1. Check the sentence that best states the main idea.

   _____ Firefighters work hard.

   _____ Firefighters live at the fire station.

   _____ We visited a fire station.

2. Number the sentences in the order they happened in the story.

   _____ The firefighters jumped on their fire trucks and drove away.

   _____ We saw the big fire trucks.

   _____ We heard a loud siren.

   _____ We put on the firefighters' coats, pants, boots, and hats.

Vocabulary Skills

Write the letter of the word or words that have the same or about the same meaning.

1. big   _____   **A.** put out

2. extinguish _____   **B.** special clothes

3. uniform   _____   **C.** tools

4. tall   _____   **D.** large

5. equipment _____   **E.** high

Language Skills

Pronouns take the place of nouns. Write who the pronoun that is underlined is referring to in each sentence.

1. <u>We</u> met Captain Jim. _____

2. <u>He</u> showed us the big fire trucks.

   _____

3. Frankie fell over when <u>he</u> put on the heavy clothes.

   _____

4. <u>We</u> got to see where the firefighters live when they are on duty.

   _____

Study Skills

Write a word that you could type in your search engine to search for more information on the Internet about each job below.

1. firefighter _____

2. police officer _____

3. paramedic _____

4. ambulance driver _____

5. doctor _____

www.summerbridgeactivities.com   © RBP Books

A Trip to the Grocery Store

Mother thought of the trip to the grocery store as a chore. Daniel thought of the trip to the grocery store as an adventure. Mother could only see the things on her list. Daniel saw the variety of things to eat.

In the produce department, Daniel counted nine different types of apples! Daniel's mother picked up one bag of Granny Smith apples. They were the type of apples she always bought. They were the family's favorite.

The cereal row was like a library filled with colorful books. Daniel enjoyed reading all of the different names. He enjoyed reading about all the different prizes inside the boxes. Daniel's mother just found the family-size box of their favorite cereal. Daniel noted

it was one of the few cereals without sugar. Daniel wondered how his mother always managed to find the one box without sugar.

In the dairy section, Daniel wondered how many cows it took to fill all the containers of milk. He wondered if the cows that gave low-fat milk were skinnier than the cows that gave the whole milk. Daniel's mother always chose two gallons of low-fat milk. Once in a while, if Daniel's mother was in a particularly good mood, she would toss some yogurt into the cart.

At the checkout stand, Daniel loved to count all the different types of gum. He wondered who would chew all the gum. Daniel's mother just worried about having enough money to pay for the groceries. For mother, the grocery store was a chore. For Daniel, it was an adventure!

Reading Skills

1. Who thought the trip to the grocery store was a chore?

_____

Why? _____

_____

_____

2. Who thought the trip to the grocery store was an adventure?

_____

Why? _____

_____

_____

Vocabulary Skills

Write the words, leaving spaces between the **syllables**.

1. adventure_____ **ad ven ture** _____

2. different _____

3. favorite _____

4. department _____

5. colorful _____

6. container _____

7. variety _____

8. particularly _____

Language Skills

Write the **base word** for each word below.

1. reading _____

2. colorful _____

3. noted _____

4. managed _____

5. skinnier _____

6. worried _____

Thinking Skills

Organize the following list in order of where you would find them in a grocery store.

milk	bagels	carrots
muffins	chicken	bananas
lettuce	hamburger	roast
hot dog buns	cheese	butter

1. dairy   **3.** breads

_____   _____

_____   _____

_____   _____

2. produce   **4.** meats

_____   _____

_____   _____

Briauna's Favorite Place

Briauna lives in Newfoundland, Canada. She is at her favorite place. It is a high cliff that overlooks the ocean. She likes to watch the fishing boats bob like corks on the blue water. She listens to the cries of the seagulls as they look for food. She admires the beauty of the tall lighthouse. She laughs as she watches the whales play. Briauna lies on her back. She finds animals in the clouds. Briauna loves to feel the mist from the ocean spray against her face. It is a peaceful day.

Suddenly, a huge wave crashes onto the shore. The fishing boats start coming to port as fast as they can. The clouds darken. A strong wind begins to blow. A foghorn cries out. It warns the seamen a storm is coming. The waves get bigger and bigger.

At first, sailors thought giant sea monsters made the waves rise high over their boats. Now they know it is the weather that causes the huge waves.

As the storm comes in, Briauna is glad she is high above the angry ocean. She takes one last look at the beautiful white-capped waves. Then she quickly runs home.

www.summerbridgeactivities.com

Reading Skills

1. What is the main idea of this story?

   A. a favorite place

   B. sailors and whales

   C. weather changes

2. What did the fishing boats look like on the ocean?

   A. bobbing corks

   B. sinking ships

   C. specks in the sea

3. A long time ago, what did sailors believe caused the waves?

   A. bad luck

   B. whales

   C. giant sea monsters

4. You can guess that _____.

   A. sailing in a storm is fun

   B. Briauna loves the sea

   C. fishing is best during a storm

Vocabulary Skills

Write the two words that make up each **compound word**.

1. overlooks _____ _____

2. seagulls _____ _____

3. lighthouse _____ _____

4. foghorn _____ _____

5. seamen _____ _____

Language Skills

Adjectives are words that describe nouns. Write the adjective from the story that describes each noun below.

1. water _____

2. lighthouse _____

3. day _____

4. wave _____

5. wind _____

6. ocean _____

Thinking Skills

The writer describes the sea using the senses. Write descriptions from the story from each of the senses below.

1. What did Briauna see?

   _____

   _____

2. What did Briauna hear?

   _____

   _____

3. What did Briauna feel?

   _____

   _____

How to Frost a Cake

Jessica is making a cake for her mother's birthday. Her grandmother helped her bake the cake. But her grandmother had to go home. She left the following directions for Jessica:

1. Remove the cake from the baking pan and put it on a plate. To do this, place a plate face down on the cake. Then flip the cake and the plate over. Remove the baking pan.

2. Open the frosting can. Spoon some frosting onto the middle of the cake.

3. Spread the frosting using the spreader. Always work from the center out to the sides. Add more frosting as needed. Spread the frosting evenly over all of the cake.

Be careful not to press too hard, or you will tear the cake.

Reading Skills

1. What is the main idea?

   A. a surprise for Mother's birthday

   B. Grandma is a good cook.

   C. frosting a cake

2. Number the directions in the right order.

   _____ Spoon frosting onto the middle of the cake.

   _____ Place the cake on a dish.

   _____ Spread the frosting.

   _____ Add more frosting.

3. What warning did Grandma give Jessica?

   A. Don't lick your fingers.

   B. Don't use too much frosting.

   C. Be careful not to press too hard.

Vocabulary Skills

1. What is the meaning of <u>directions</u> in this story?

   A. north, south, east, and west

   B. steps to finish frosting the cake

   C. a map to someone's house

2. What is a <u>spreader</u>?

   A. a tool used to spread frosting

   B. a knife for cutting bread

   C. a tool for making the bed

Study Skills

Read the recipe. Answer the questions below.

Vanilla Frosting

3 cups powdered sugar

1/3 cup butter, softened

1 tsp vanilla

1 TBS milk

1. Mix butter and sugar together. Stir in vanilla and milk. Beat until smooth.

2. Spread on cake.

Makes enough frosting for one 13 x 9-inch cake.

1. How many cups of powered sugar do you need? _____

2. Do you need more milk or more vanilla? _____

3. How long are you supposed to beat the frosting? _____

4. Do you need more or less than 1 cup of butter? _____

Thinking Skills

1. What is your favorite kind of cake? What frosting goes best with it? Why?

   _____

   _____

   _____

   _____

"Happy Mother's Day," Nathan said. Nathan gave his mother a large box with a pretty bow.

"What is it?" his mother asked. "You have to guess," Nathan said. "I'll give you a hint. It's soft and blue."

"Can I wear it?" asked his mother.

"Yes," said Nathan.

"I think I know," his mother said. She opened the box. "Thank you. It is just what I asked for," she said.

Nathan's mother took the gift out of the box. She put it on over her head. She put her arms in the sleeves. It fit just right. Nathan's mother gave him a big hug.

www.summerbridgeactivities.com Reading Connection—Grade 2—RBP3810

Reading Skills

1. What did Nathan give his mother?

A. a blanket

B. a pair of slippers

C. a sweater

2. Why did Nathan give his mother a present?

A. It was Mother's Day.

B. It was her birthday.

C. His mother had been sick.

3. What did Mother give Nathan?

A. a present

B. a hug

C. a sweater

Vocabulary Skills

A **homonym** (or **homophone**) is a word that sounds the same but is spelled differently and has a different meaning. Draw a line between the homonyms.

1. wear   ewe

2. him   blew

3. you   where

4. blue   no

5. know   hymn

Language Skills

The words it, she, and he take the place of a person or thing in a sentence. Answer the questions about these sentences.

1. He gave her a large box. Who is he?

_____

2. She opened the box. Who is she?

_____

3. She put it on over her head. What is

it? _____

Thinking Skills

Answer these riddles.

1. What is read and has pages?

_____

2. What barks and is man's best friend?

_____

3. What is orange, round, and sweet?

_____

4. What has eight legs and lives in the

sea? _____

The Birthday Present Mix-Up

Today is Rachel's birthday. She invited four friends to her party. Each friend brought a present. Rachel's little brother mixed up the tags on the presents. Can you use the clues to put the tags on the right presents?

Kelly's present has flowered wrapping paper and a bow.

Kate's present is square and has a bow.

Meg forgot the bow on her present.

Lisa's present has striped wrapping paper.

Put an **X** in the box when you know a present does not belong to one of the girls. Put **O** when you know a present belongs to one of the girls.

	Square, striped with bow	Square, flowered with bow	Square, flowered without bow	Rectangle, striped with bow
Kate				
Kelly				
Lisa				
Meg				

www.summerbridgeactivities.com

Reading Skills

1. What event is happening in the story?
   A. Rachel's birthday party
   B. Meg's birthday party
   C. Friendship Day

2. Put a **T** by the sentences that are true. Put an **F** by the sentences that are false.

   _____ Kate's present has a bow.

   _____ Meg's present has a bow.

   _____ Kelly's present has striped wrapping paper.

   _____ Lisa forgot to bring a present.

   _____ Rachel's little brother is helpful.

Language Skills

An **apostrophe** (')is used to show possession. Circle the word that needs an apostrophe in each sentence below. Write the word correctly on the line.

1. Rachels brother is three years old.

   _____

2. Kates present has a big bow.

   _____

3. My brothers friend spent the night.

   _____

4. Each presents tag was missing.

   _____

5. Lisas present has striped paper.

   _____

Vocabulary Skills

1. Draw a picture of a present. Write a sentence describing the present.

   _____

   _____

   _____

   _____

2. Write the name of each girl (Kelly, Kate, Meg, Lisa) under the present she brought.

   _____   _____

   _____   _____

Pet Show

Today is the day of the neighbor-hood pet show. Holly, Amanda, Nico, and Nathan have brought their pets. See if you can match each child to his or her pet.

Nathan's pet likes to chase the girl's cat.

Holly's pet sings from its perch.

Nico's pet runs around on a wheel in its cage.

Put an **X** in the box when you know an animal does not belong to a child. Put an **O** when you know an animal does belong.

	Cat	Dog	Hamster	Bird
Holly				
Amanda				
Nico				
Nathan				

www.summerbridgeactivities.com

Reading Connection—Grade 2—RBP3810

Reading Skills

1. What event is happening in the story?

A. school fair

B. pet show

C. circus

2. Draw a line from the children to their pets.

Holly   cat

Amanda   dog

Nico   hamster

Nathan   bird

3. Write the pet under what it does.

A. sings from its perch

_____

B. runs around in its cage

_____

C. chases the cat

_____

Language Skills

To show ownership, use **'s** after a name. Use the names from the story to complete the sentences below. Use *'s*.

1. _____ cat is named Whiskers.

2. _____ dog is black and white.

3. _____ hamster is small and brown.

4. _____ bird can say, "Hello."

Thinking Skills

1. Put an **X** by the animals that would not make good pets.

_____ elephant

_____ rabbit

_____ lion

_____ giraffe

_____ fish

_____ dog

2. Which pet would make the best pet?

_____

Why?

_____

_____

_____

Who's the Pitcher?

In our neighborhood we have a family of quintuplets. Quintuplets are sort of like twins, except instead of two there are five. The quintuplets' names are Nan, Stan, Dan, Jan, and Van. Today the whole neighborhood is playing baseball. One of the quintuplets is the pitcher. The pitcher is wearing sunglasses and a striped shirt. The pitcher wears a glove on his or her left hand. Which quintuplet is the pitcher?

Stan

Nan

Jan

Dan

Van

www.summerbridgeactivities.com

Reading Connection—Grade 2—RBP3810

Reading Skills

1. Who is the pitcher?

_____

2. Put a **T** by the sentences that are true. Put an **F** by the sentences that are false.

_____ Nan is not wearing sunglasses.

_____ Dan is wearing a striped shirt.

_____ Stan forgot his sunglasses.

_____ Jan has her glove on the right hand.

_____ Van is the pitcher.

Thinking Skills

Cross out the word that does not belong in each group.

1. twins   triplets
    babies   quadruplets

2. pitcher   quarterback
    catcher   outfielder

3. Nan   Stan
    Jan   Bob

4. racket   bat
    ball   glove

Vocabulary Skills

1. What does <u>quintuplets</u> mean?

  A. many children born on the same day to the same mother

  B. five children born on the same day to the same mother

  C. twins born on the same day to the same mother

2. Write three words that rhyme with the quintuplets' names.

_____

_____

_____

Write the **compound word**.

3. glasses worn in the sun

_____

4. ball game played with bases

_____

5. a box for mail

_____

For one year I have been writing to a pen pal. A pen pal is a friend that you write to. My pen pal's name is Max. He is in the second grade. He lives in Canada with his family. Today Max is coming for a visit. I am going to meet him at the airport. I have never seen Max, so I'm not sure what he looks like. Max said to look for a boy with curly hair and glasses. Max said he would be wearing a baseball cap and carrying a backpack. Can you help me find Max?

www.summerbridgeactivities.com   **Reading Connection—Grade 2—RBP3810**

Reading Skills

1. Circle Max in the picture on the other side.

2. What is a pen pal?

   A. a friend that you write to

   B. a cousin who lives far away

   C. a person from Canada

3. How long has the writer been writing to Max?

   A. one month

   B. one year

   C. two years

4. Why doesn't the writer know what Max looks like?

   A. He forgot.

   B. Max looks different.

   C. He has never seen Max.

5. Put a **T** by the things that are true about Max. Put an **N** by things that are not true. Put a **U** by the things you don't know.

   _____ Max has curly hair.

   _____ Max is in the third grade.

   _____ Max has a dog.

   _____ Max wears glasses.

   _____ Max lives in the United States.

   _____ Max likes to play soccer.

Vocabulary Skills

Write the two little words that make up each of these **compound words**.

1. airport   _____   _____

2. baseball   _____   _____

3. backpack   _____   _____

4. mailbox   _____   _____

5. sunglasses   _____   _____

Thinking Skills

1. Pretend you have a pen pal. Write a short letter to your pen pal below.

   _____

   _____

   _____

   _____

   _____

   _____

   _____

   _____

   _____

   _____

Where Is Jeff?

My friend Jeff loves to play games.
Hide-and-seek is his favorite game.
Today he left me this note:

Dear Brian,

Want to play hide-and-seek?
Follow the directions to find me!

Start at your house.
Go east on Maple Street to Elm Street.
Go south on Elm Street to Apple Way.
Go west on Apple Way to Willow Road.
Go south on Willow Road.
Stop at the first building.

Hope to see you soon.

Your friend,
Jeff

Follow the directions in the
note to help me find Jeff.

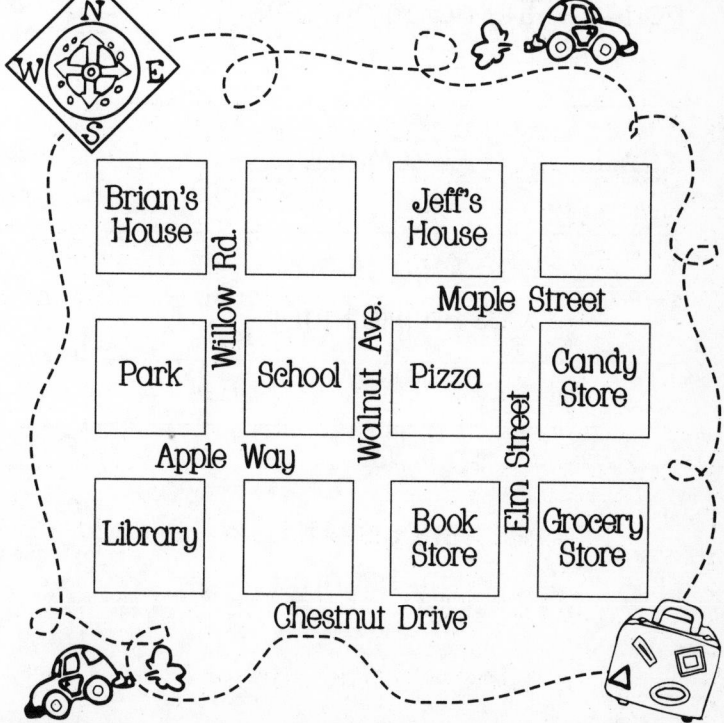

Reading Skills

1. Where is Jeff hiding?

_____

2. What is Jeff's favorite game?
   A. baseball
   B. hide-and-seek
   C. soccer

3. What is the name of Jeff's friend?

_____

Language Skills

1. Proper nouns are specific persons, places, or things. Proper nouns begin with a capital letter. List all the proper nouns in the note from Jeff.

_____

_____

_____

_____

Vocabulary Skills

1. Circle the words that mean the same as <u>street</u>.

road	way
tree	avenue
garden	drive

Thinking Skills

Cross out the word that doesn't belong in each group.

1. elm   maple
    apple   daisy

2. apple   banana
    carrot   strawberry

3. red   orange
    apple   blue

4. Jeff   Bryan
    Nathan   Rachel

5. north   south
    left   west

6. What are all the streets in the story named after?

_____

Treasure Map

Ben and Matt were playing pirates. While digging for treasure, they found this map. Follow the directions to find the treasure.

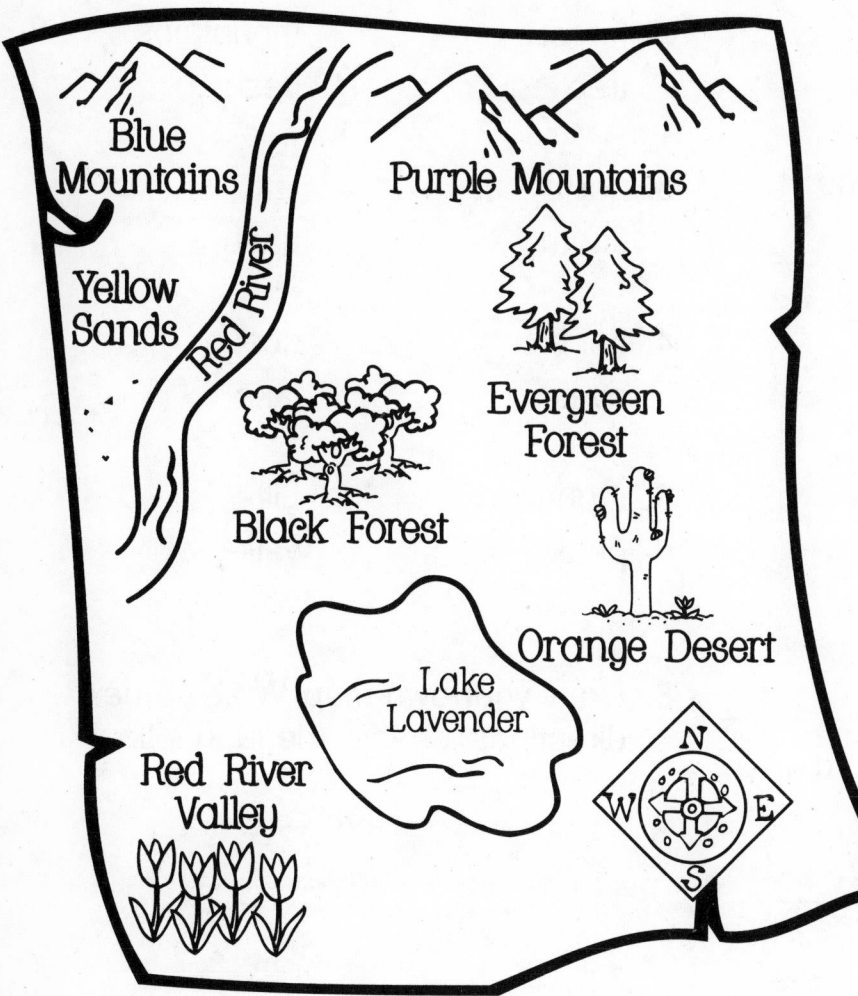

Start in the Red River Valley.

Go north to the Black Forest.

Go east to the next forest.

Travel north to the Purple Mountains.

Cross the Red River to the Blue Mountains.

Go south, but do not cross the Red River again.

The treasure is buried here.

Reading Skills

1. Where is the treasure buried?

_____

2. When you go east from the Black Forest, what forest do you find?

_____

3. Draw a line from the color to the place as noted on the map.

yellow   mountains

orange   river

red   sands

purple   desert

Language Skills

Write the **base word** for each word below.

1. playing _____

2. digging _____

3. buried _____

4. missing _____

5. hunting _____

Thinking Skills

Cross out the word that doesn't belong in each group.

1. blue   yellow
    red   sky

2. forest   mountains
    tree   desert

3. north   left
    south   east

4. desert   ocean
    river   lake

5. mountain   hill
    peak   valley

6. Draw your own map. Write some directions for your friend to follow.

_____

_____

_____

_____

Reading Connection—Grade 2—RBP3810   www.summerbridgeactivities.com   ©RBP Books

The Great Race

Find a friend and play this game.

What You Will Need:
Coin
Markers

Object of the Game:
To be the first to cross the finish line

How to Play:
The youngest player goes first.
Flip a coin. Move 1 space for heads. Move 2 spaces for tails.
Follow the directions on each space.

Start ⚙	Slow start. Go back 1 space.	Great start! Go ahead 2 spaces.			Tripped on shoelace. Go back 1 space.	⚙
⚙			Running strong. Take another turn.			⚙
⚙	Record time. Go ahead 3 spaces.		Leg cramps. Lose a turn.			⚙
⚙				Getting tired. Rest 1 turn.		⚙
⚙	Missed a hurdle. Go back 2 spaces.					Finish

Reading Skills

1. What is the main idea?

    A. how to play a game

    B. how to run in a race

    C. how to be in first place

2. Match each action with the consequence.

A. tripped on shoelace	go back 2 spaces
B. getting tired	win the game
C. missed a hurdle	go back 1 space
D. flipped coin is heads	move ahead 1 space
E. flipped coin is tails	move ahead 2 spaces
F. cross the finish line first	rest 1 turn

3. Who goes first?

    A. the person who has the game

    B. the biggest person

    C. the youngest person

4. What is the object of the game?

    A. to not trip when running a race

    B. to be the first to cross the finish line

    C. to get the best start

Language Skills

Write the **base word** for the following words:

1. tripped _____

2. running _____

3. missed _____

4. getting _____

5. flipped _____

6. tired _____

7. crossed _____

8. going _____

Study Skills

Read this game box. Answer the questions.

> A Rainbow Bridge Game
>
> # HOP TO IT!
>
> **The game that keeps you on your toes.**
>
> For 3 or more players
> For ages 5 to adult

1. What is the name of the game?

_____

2. How old do you need to be to play the game? _____

3. Can two people play the game? _____

Reading Connection—Grade 2—RBP3810   www.summerbridgeactivities.com   ©RBP Books

Page 8

Reading Skills
1. C
2. A
3. C

Thinking Skills
1. computer, maps, video tapes, encyclopedias, couch

Vocabulary Skills
1. more, Answers will vary.
2. quietly, Answers will vary.
3. anyplace, Answers will vary.
4. be, Answers will vary.

Language Skills
1. read
2. saw
3. took
4. came

Page 10

Reading Skills
1. A
2. winter/basketball, spring/soccer, summer/baseball, fall/football

Vocabulary Skills
1. good at sports
2. a good sport

Language Skills
1. shoot
2. kick
3. hit
4. run

Thinking Skills
1. hoop
2. football
3. baseball
4. bat

Page 12

Reading Skills
1. A
2. 2, 5, 1, 3, 4
3. A

Vocabulary Skills
1. snow   man
2. snow   ball
3. pine   cone
4. out   side

Language Skills
1. days
2. snowmen
3. sticks
4. snowballs
5. pinecones

Thinking Skills
1. Answers will vary.

Page 14

Reading Skills
1. A
2. C
3. B

Vocabulary Skills
1. grows rows
   gold   behold
   seen   green
   along song
   see   me
2. C

Language Skills
1. daisy
2. bee
3. butterfly
4. buttercup
5. grass

Thinking Skills
1. oak tree
2. grasses
3. meadow

Answer Pages

Page 16

Reading Skills
1. B
2. A
3. B

Vocabulary Skills
1. B
2. <u>or</u> words: colors, oranges, for, forth
   <u>ir</u> word: birds
   <u>er</u> word: flower
   <u>ar</u> words: garden, are

Study Skills
1. 26
2. 31
3. 15
4. 19

Page 18

Reading Skills
1. B
2. sight   storm clouds moving in
   touch   tiny sprinkles on my face
   taste   little drops inside my mouth
   sound   tapping on the window
   smell   fresh air

Vocabulary Skills
1. begin   in
2. face   chase
3. wide   inside
4. window know
5. green   clean

Language Skills
1. moving
2. playing
3. letting
4. tapping

Thinking Skills
1. The writer loves the rain.

Page 20

Reading Skills
1. C
2. B
3. A

Vocabulary Skills
1. B
2. A. spring   time
   B. them   selves
   C. blue   bird
   D. winter   time

Thinking Skills
1. snow boots   coat   scarf
2. swimsuit   shorts   sandals
3. raincoat   galoshes   sweater
4. jacket   new school clothes   football jersey

Study Skills
1. seasons   animals   change
   (or any reasonable answer)

Page 22

Reading Skills
1. A
2. C
3. play outside, go swimming, ride bikes, go to the park

Vocabulary Skills
1. sun   shine
2. out   side
3. rain drop
4. class room

Language Skills
1. noun
2. verb
3. verb
4. noun
5. verb
6. noun

Thinking Skills
1. winter: sledding, snow, mittens
2. spring: flowers, baby animals, rain
3. summer: swimming, hot weather, shorts
4. fall: football, leaves falling, school starts

Answer Pages

Page 24

Reading Skills
1. A
2. It is sweet.
   The lemonade has lots of ice.
   You have time.

Language Skills
1. it will
2. it is
3. you have
4. I have
5. we have

Vocabulary Skills
1. A
2. B

Thinking Skills
   Answers will vary.

Page 26

Reading Skills
1. C
2. A. my big sister
   B. Mom
   C. Dad
   D. my little brother

Vocabulary Skills
1. dish   fish
   wig   pig
   hat   cat
   log   dog

Language Skills
1. "Let's go shopping," said Mother.
2. "Can we buy a pet?" asked my brother.
3. "We don't need a pet," said my father.
4. "That dog needs a home," said my mother.
5. "Okay," said my father, "we can buy the dog."

Study Skills
1. collie
2. Sam
3. $50.00
4. 446-2111

Page 28

Reading Skills
1. a cat
2. a big cat with black spots
3. The person saw it last week.

Vocabulary Skills
1. big   little
   stripes   spots
   white   black
   fast   slow

Thinking Skills
1. Because the other person didn't know where it was.

Language Skills
1. o   3. a
2. i   4. a

Study Skills
1. A lost cat
2. Rachel
3. 448-8888
4. something given as a thank you (Accept any reasonable answer.)

Page 30

Reading Skills
1. F
2. T
3. F
4. T
5. B

Language Skills
1. swim
2. fly
3. learn
4. swing
5. be
6. have

Thinking Skills
1. Answers will vary.

Study Skills
1. 5   4. 17
2. 2   5. 14
3. 10   6. 3

Page 32

Reading Skills
1. C
2. 3, 2, 4, 1, 5

Vocabulary Skills
1. kicked
2. roll
3. cried
4. clap

Language Skills
1. tromp
2. swing
3. hop
4. slither
5. grin

Study Skills
1. paw
2. moan
3. animal
4. bison

Page 34

Reading Skills
1. B
2. 4, 1, 3, 2
3. B

Vocabulary Skills
1. o
2. i
3. a
4. u

Language Skills
1. noun
2. verb
3. noun
4. verb
5. noun
6. verb

Study Skills
1. 3, 4, 1, 2
2. 3, 1, 4, 2
3. 4, 3, 1, 2
4. 3, 1, 4, 2

Page 36

Reading Skills
1. B
2. C
3. She got the idea to sell the birdhouses.
   She made posters.
   She hung the posters around the neighborhood.
4. 2 1 4 3 5

Vocabulary Skills
1. make   made
2. hang   hung
3. give   gave
4. build   built
5. sell   sold

Study Skills
1. bird*house
2. beau*ti*ful
3. pos*ter
4. dol*lar
5. busi*ness

Page 38

Reading Skills
1. A
2. B
3. A. robin   cherry tree
   B. magpie   pine tree
   C. quail   under a bush

Vocabulary Skills
1. A

Language Skills
1. peek
2. count
3. family
4. watch
5. place

Study Skills
I   3. build nests in cherry tree
II 1. shiny black feathers
    4. noisy birds
III 2. make nests under a bush

Page 40

Reading Skills

1. B
2.
horse	gallops
kangaroo	hops
duck	waddles
fish	swims
birds	fly
snake	slithers

Vocabulary Skills

1. u
2. o
3. i
4. i

Thinking Skills

1.
<u>two feet</u>:	chicken, penguin
<u>four feet</u>:	cat, deer
<u>flies</u>:	robin, owl
<u>swims</u>:	whale, goldfish

Page 42

Reading Skills

1. A
2. Insects have three main body parts.
   Insects have six legs.
   Insects have feelers on their heads.

Vocabulary Skills

1. B
2. C
3. A
4. D

Language Skills

1. a
2. i
3. a

Study Skills

1. The Interesting World of Insects
2. Joshua Ryan
3. Rainbow Bridge Publishing
4. Salt Lake City, Utah

Page 44

Reading Skills

1. C
2. B
3. A
4. **C**

Vocabulary Skills

1. B
2. B

Language Skills

1. California, United States, Australia

Study Skills

1. 5 1 6 3 4 2 7

Page 46

Reading Skills

1. B
2. An ant can carry things twice its size.
   Ants use feelers to help them find food.
   An ant's jaw opens sideways.

Language Skills

1. ant
2. ants

Vocabulary Skills

1. A

Study Skills

1. 4
2. Ant Families
3. 26
4. All About Ants

Answer Pages

Page 48

Reading Skills
1. B
2. A
3. B

Vocabulary Skills
1. A   2. B

Language Skills
1. koalas   4. babies
2. marsupials   5. bears
3. pouches   6. leaves

Study Skills
1. koala, marsupial, Australia (Answers may vary.)
2. Answers will vary. Possibilities: bandicoot, feathertail glider, wallaroo, wallaby, wombat, quokka, numbat, opossum, Tasmanian devil, marsupial cat, marsupial mole, marsupial mouse, marsupial rat

Page 50

Reading Skills
1. C   2. T, F, F, T

Vocabulary Skills
1. harmful   helpful
   truth   myth
   afraid   brave
   wild   tame
2. A

Language Skills
1. is   4. is
2. are   5. are
3. are

Study Skills
 I B. other pests
 II A. Hair
 II B. Suck blood

Thinking Skills
1. Answers will vary.

Page 52

Reading Skills
1. A
2. Wash your hands with soap.
   Cover your mouth when you cough or sneeze.
   Get plenty of sleep.
   Eat healthy meals.
3. T, F, T, T, F

Language Skills
1. i
2. u
3. u
4. o

Study Skills
1. noun
2. 1
3. after
4. Accept any reasonable sentence.

Page 54

Reading Skills
1. Stamp collecting is a fun & interesting hobby.
2. stamps, an album, tweezers, plastic pages

Language Skills
1. collect
2. supply
3. organize
4. damp

Vocabulary Skills
1. a stamp collector
2. tweezers   to handle the stamps
3. plastic pages   to protect the stamps
4. albums   to organize the pages
5. cool, dry place to keep the albums safe from heat, sun, and dampness

Study Skills
 I. A. tweezers, B. plastic pages, C. album
 II. A. new stamps, B. used stamps
 III. A. by value, B. by location, C. by theme

Page 56

Reading Skills
1. B
2. C
3. A

Vocabulary Skills
1. scrap book
2. head line
3. some thing
4. every one
5. book store
6. B
7. memories, mementos, remember

Language Skills
1. store
2. memory
3. supply
4. organize
5. write
6. erase

Page 58

Reading Skills
1. F
2. T
3. T
4. F

Vocabulary Skills
1. B
2. B

Language Skills
1. November 15, 2001.
2. pizza, popcorn, pretzels, and pickles.
3. There's a Nightmare in My Closet, There's an Alligator under My Bed, and Terrible Troll.
4. A Boy, a Dog, and a Frog.
5. December 30, 1943.

Study Skills
1. 1
2. 6
3. 11
4. 3

Page 60

Reading Skills
1. Sammy is one of the greatest baseball players.
2. playing baseball
3. F, F, T, T, T

Language Skills
1. base ball
2. card board
3. great
4. grow
5. roll
6. high
7. value

Vocabulary Skills
1. E
2. A
3. D
4. C
5. B

Study Skills
1. C
2. A
3. E
4. D
5. B

Page 62

Reading Skills
1. A
2. The writer likes grass and trees.

Thinking Skills
1.

Alike or Different?	grass	tree
living thing	X	X
stands straight in the wind		X
bends in the wind	X	
tall		X
small	X	
Mother Nature's gift	X	X
you can climb it		X
you can pick it up	X	
green in color	X	X

Vocabulary Skills
1. tall   small   wall
2. gift   lift   sift
3. spring   sing   thing
4. bent
5. small
6. sit

Study Skills
1. blossoms
2. knot
3. roots
4. branches

Page 64

Reading Skills
1. A
2. B
3. B

Vocabulary Skills
1. A
2. C

Thinking Skills
1.

Alike or Different?	Chris	Will
Born on December 22	X	X
Has red curly hair and blue eyes		X
Has straight brown hair and green eyes	X	
In the second grade	X	X
In Miss Blinn's class	X	
Good at reading	X	X
A good artist	X	
A good ball player		X

Study Skills
1. twins, fraternal, identical twins (Answers may vary.)

Page 66

Reading Skills
1. C
2. sister
3. brother
4. sister
5. brother
6. sister
7. brother

Vocabulary Skills
1. brown eyes   blue eyes
2. sit   stand
3. sunburn   tan
4. quiet   loud
5. humble   proud

Language Skills
1. but
2. and
3. but
4. and

Thinking Skills
1. Answers will vary.
2. Answers will vary.

Page 68

Reading Skills
1. A
2. A
3. B

Language Skills
1. Answers will vary.

Vocabulary Skills
1. bear   there
2. kid   hid
3. friend   pretend
4. sleep   sheep
5. so   go
6. bed   Ted
7. me   see
8. I   am
9. it   is
10. could   not
11. I   have

Thinking Skills
1. Answers will vary.

Page 70

Thinking Skills
1. A
2. B
3. C

Vocabulary Skills
1. him
2. son
3. road
4. weak
5. break
6. eight
7. pear
8. blue
9. knight
10. sea

Language Skills
1. ate
2. sun
3. blue
4. pair
5. road

Study Skills
1. 3, 4, 1, 2
2. 2, 1, 4, 3
3. 3, 4, 2, 1

Answer Pages

Page 72

Reading Skills
1. C

Vocabulary Skills
1. talk   chatter
2. walk   stroll
3. run   dash
4. jump   leap
5. laugh   giggle
6. sleep   snooze
7. whisper
8. march
9. dash
10. cackle
11. slumber
12. chuckled

Study Skills
1. no
2. it's an adjective
3. Accept any reasonable answer.

Thinking Skills
1. Answers will vary. They may include large, enormous, huge, gigantic, colossal.

Page 74

Reading Skills
1. F
2. F
3. T
4. T
5. She always said and did the opposite.

Vocabulary Skills
1. south
2. adorable
3. white
4. back
5. wet
6. full

Language Skills
1. began
2. thought
3. said
4. rode
5. sat

Study Skills
1. monkeys
2. snakes
3. birds
4. giraffes

Page 76

Reading Skills
1. The PTA Challenge: Our Goal Is 100% Membership!
2. 100% membership
3. Miss Sloan's
4. Mrs. Carter's
5. Miss Casaday's and Ms. Thomas's

Vocabulary Skills
1. married woman
2. man
3. doctor, man or woman
4. unmarried woman
5. woman, married or unmarried

Language Skills
1. Mrs. Simmons's
2. Ms. Sloan's
3. Ms. Turner's, Mr. Gomez's
4. Miss Casaday's

Study Skills
1. yes
2. no
3. yes
4. no
5. no

Page 78

Reading Skills
1. A
2. C
3. A
4. C

Vocabulary Skills
1. food (it's not a verb)
2. clown (it doesn't rhyme)
3. laugh (it's not a synonym of talk)
4. know (it's the opposite of the other words)
5. serious (it's the opposite of the other words)

Language Skills
1. shopping
2. decorating
3. eating
4. laughing
5. cooking

Study Skills
1. 2, 1, 4, 3

Page 80

Reading Skills
1. A
2. exit—D
   train tracks—C
   girls' bathroom—F
   be careful—H
   boys' bathroom—E
   enter here—G
   stop—A
   yield the right way—B

Vocabulary Skills
1. stop   go
2. boy   girl
3. enter   exit
4. everywhere nowhere
5. careful   careless

Thinking Skills
1. Answers will vary.

Page 82

Reading Skills
1. C
2. adults $7.50
   children $5.00
   children two and under   Free
3. The circus will be in town on June 20.
   There will be clowns at the circus.
   You can see the circus at either 3:00 or 7:00.

Language Skills
1. S
2. N
3. S
4. N
5. S

Thinking Skills
1. Circus Animals: elephant tiger lion
   Farm Animals: pig cow chicken

Page 84

Reading Skills
1. They provide warnings.
   They give first aid instructions.
   They tell how to use the product.
2. Note, warning, danger, poison, keep out of reach of children, or caution

Vocabulary Skills
1. antonym
2. synonym
3. antonym
4. antonym
5. antonym
6. synonym

Language Skills
1. Danger! Do Not Enter!
2. Run and get help!
3. Today is Saturday.
4. Don't touch the hot stove!
5. My brother is 3 years older than me.

Study Skills
1. Clean EZ
2. cleaning kitchen appliances, windows, countertops, bathroom fixtures, and mirrors
3. ammonia
4. Keep out of reach of children.
5. 800-555-1555
6. no

Page 86

Reading Skills
1. Josh
2. birthday
3. September 13
4. Papa's Pizza Palace
5. September 10

Vocabulary Skills
1. C
2. A
3. B

Language Skills
1. C
2. P
3. C
4. P

Study Skills
1. Spy Tools
2. 32–39
3. The Job of a Spy
4. 13

Answer Pages

Page 88

Reading Skills
1. Grandma and Grandpa
2. Nick
3. Accept any reasonable answer.

Vocabulary Skills
1. C
2. D
3. E
4. A
5. B

Language Skills
1. what is
2. I am
3. we are
4. can not
5. you will
6. I will

Thinking Skills
1. Answers will vary.

Page 90

Reading Skills
1. B
2. C
3. A
4. B
5. A

Vocabulary Skills
1. one
2. dear
3. some
4. two
5. days
6. blew
7. so
8. rains

Language Skills
1. mice
2. acorns
3. houses
4. years
5. days

Study Skills
1. Aesop, fables

Page 92

Reading Skills
1. D
2. A
3. B
4. A

Vocabulary Skills
1. huge
2. pull
3. little
4. move
5. whole
6. shove

Language Skills
1. came
2. fed
3. started
4. went
5. said
6. took
7. moved
8. broke

Page 94

Reading Skills
1. B
2. C
3. T
4. T
5. F
6. F
7. T

Vocabulary Skills
1. hours
2. reel
3. week
4. be
5. threw

Language Skills
1. ?
2. !
3. .
4. ?
5. .

Thinking Skills
1. Answers will vary.

www.summerbridgeactivities.com

Page 96

Reading Skills
1. 8 2 1 3 7 4 5 6

Vocabulary Skills
1. sighed screamed shouted squealed bellowed snickered

Study Skills
1. Gingerbread Cookies
2. 6
3. ginger, allspice, cinnamon
4. 350 degrees
5. overnight
6. 10 – 12 minutes
7. 2 dozen

Page 98

Reading Skills
1. Once up a time, in a kingdom far away…
   Pepper ate only pickled potato pancakes.
   The castle was painted a pleasant shade of pink.
   They lived happily ever after.

Vocabulary Skills
1. hunted
2. laughed
3. shouted
4. pretty
5. questioned

Language Skills
1–4. Answers will vary.

Study Skills
1. 12
2. 3
3. 13
4. 8

Page 100

Reading Skills
1. B
2. C
3. B

Language Skills
1. is
2. are
3. are
4. are
5. is

Vocabulary Skills
1. B
2. B
3. unkind, mean, uncaring, heartless, harsh

Thinking Skills
1. Answers will vary.

Page 102

Reading Skills
1. rivers, trees, cattle, garden, roof
2. A. blue air
   B. green garden
   C. brown roof
3. No answers necessary.

Language Skills
1. up
2. on
3. over
4. down
5. in
6. brown
7. do
8. wall
9. swing

Vocabulary Skills
1. biggest
2. longest
3. prettiest
4. nicest
5. littlest

Study Skills
1. Stevenson

Answer Pages

Page 104

Reading Skills
1. B
2. C
3. C

Vocabulary Skills
1. B
2. A

Language Skills
1. sky
2. grass
3. hid
4. all
5. old
6. me

Thinking Skills
1–3. Answers will vary.

Page 106

Reading Skills
1. C
2. B
3. A

Vocabulary Skills
1. grand mother
2. half way
3. ball park
4. water slide
5. play ground

Language Skills
1. V, N
2. V, N
3. V, N
4. V, N
5. N, V

Thinking Skills
1. Answers will vary.

Page 108

Reading Skills
1. B
2. playing basketball, eating ice cream, running, talking, hearing stories, being tucked in
3. S U I U S I

Vocabulary Skills
1. stories
2. kisses
3. hugs
4. friends
5. cones
6. neighbors
7. boys
8. girls

Language Skills
1. basket ball
2. bed time
3. fore head
4. some times

Thinking Skills
1. Answers will vary.

Page 110

Reading Skills
1. B
2. 2, 1, 5, 3, 4
3. S B B S S B

Vocabulary Skills
1. er
2. est
3. er
4. est

Study Skills
1. 6
2. 2
3. 15
4. 15
5. 7

© RBP Books   www.summerbridgeactivities.com   Reading Connection—Grade 2—RBP3810

Answer Pages

Page 112

Reading Skills
1. A
2. 3, 1, 2, 4, 5

Vocabulary Skills
1. big, huge, enormous, large
2. Accept any reasonable answer.
3. small tiny minute little
   (Accept any reasonable answer.)

Language Skills
1. .
2. ?
3. ?
4. .
5. ?

Thinking Skills
1. cookie divided into sixteen pieces

Page 114

Reading Skills
1. B
2. A
3. B
4. B
5. the size of the pet
   where you will keep the pet
   how much care the pet needs

Language Skills
1. it is
2. let us
3. it will
4. I am
5. do not

Thinking Skills
1. Answers will vary.

Page 116

Reading Skills
1. A
2. 3, 1, 2, 4

Language Skills
1. walk
2. pulls
3. picks
4. ride
5. see
6. tells
7. laugh
8. grow

Vocabulary Skills
1. hayride
2. barnyard
3. applesauce
4. doghouse
5. henhouse
6. bedroom

Thinking Skills
1. sheep, horse, chickens, cows
2. Answers will vary.

Page 118

Reading Skills
1. A
2. C
3. baby gorillas   roll down the hill
   giraffes   nibble leaves
   flamingos   stand on one foot
4. C
5. C

Vocabulary Skills
1. B
2. A
3. B

Thinking Skills
1. Answers will vary.

Page 120

Reading Skills
1. We visited a fire station.
2. 4, 1, 3, 2

Vocabulary Skills
1. D
2. A
3. B
4. E
5. C

Language Skills
1. the class
2. Captain Jim
3. Frankie
4. the class

Study Skills
1–5. Answers will vary.

Page 122

Reading Skills
1. mother, accept any reasonable answer
2. Daniel, accept any reasonable answer

Vocabulary Skills
1. ad ven ture
2. dif fer ent
3. fav or ite
4. de part ment
5. col or ful
6. con tain er
7. var i e ty
8. par tic u lar ly

Language Skills
1. read
2. color
3. note
4. manage
5. skinny
6. worry

Thinking Skills
1. milk   butter   cheese
2. lettuce   banana   carrots
3. hot dog buns   bagels   muffins
4. hamburger   roast   chicken

Page 124

Reading Skills
1. A
2. A
3. C
4. B

Vocabulary Skills
1. over looks
2. sea gulls
3. light house
4. fog horn
5. sea men

Language Skills
1. blue
2. tall
3. peaceful
4. huge
5. strong
6. angry

Thinking Skills
1–3. Answers will vary.

Page 126

Reading Skills
1. C
2. 2, 1, 3, 4
3. C

Vocabulary Skills
1. B
2. A

Study Skills
1. 3
2. milk
3. until smooth
4. less

Thinking Skills
1. Answers will vary.

Answer Pages

Page 128

Reading Skills
1. C
2. A
3. B

Vocabulary Skills
1. wear   where
2. him   hymn
3. you   ewe
4. blue   blew
5. know   no

Language Skills
1. Nathan
2. Mother
3. a sweater

Thinking Skills
1. book
2. dog
3. orange
4. octopus

Page 130

Reading Skills
1. A
2. T, F, F, F, F

Language Skills
1. Rachel's
2. Kate's
3. brother's
4. present's
5. Lisa's

Vocabulary Skills
1. Answers will vary.
2. Kelly   square flowered with bow
   Kate   square striped with bow
   Meg   square flowered without bow
   Lisa   rectangle striped with bow

Page 132

Reading Skills
1. B
2. Holly   bird
   Amanda   cat
   Nico   hamster
   Nathan   dog
3. A. bird
   B. hamster
   C. dog

Language Skills
1. Amanda's
2. Nathan's
3. Nico's
4. Holly's

Thinking Skills
1. elephant, lion, giraffe
2. Answers will vary.

Page 134

Reading Skills
1. Dan
2. T, T, F, T, F

Thinking Skills
1. babies
2. quarterback
3. Bob
4. racket

Vocabulary Skills
1. B
2. Answers will vary.
3. sunglasses
4. baseball
5. mailbox

Page 136

Reading Skills
1.

2. A
3. B
4. C
5. T, N, U, T, N, U

Vocabulary Skills
1. air   port
2. base   ball
3. back   pack
4. mail   box
5. sun   glasses

Thinking Skills
1. Answers will vary.

Page 138

Reading Skills
1. library
2. B
3. Brian

Language Skills
1. Brian, Maple Street, Elm Street, Apple Way, Willow Road, Jeff

Vocabulary Skills
1. road, way, avenue, drive

Thinking Skills
1. daisy
2. carrot
3. apple
4. Rachel
5. left
6. trees

Page 140

Reading Skills
1. Yellow Sands
2. Evergreen Forest
3. yellow   sands
   orange   desert
   red   river
   purple   mountains

Language Skills
1. play
2. dig
3. bury
4. miss
5. hunt

Thinking Skills
1. sky
2. tree
3. left
4. desert
5. valley
6. Answers will vary.

Page 142

Reading Skills
1. A
2. tripped on shoelace   go back 1 space
   getting tired   rest 1 turn
   missed a hurdle   go back 2 spaces
   flipped coin is head   move 1 space
   flipped coin is tails   move 2 spaces
   cross the finish line first win
3. C
4. B

Language Skills
1. trip
2. run
3. miss
4. get
5. flip
6. tire
7. cross
8. go

Study Skills
1. Hop to it!
2. 5 years old
3. no

Notes

Five things I'm thankful for:

1. _____
2. _____
3. _____
4. _____
5. _____